ORDER OUT OF CHAOS

A Relationship with Alzheimer's Disease
born of
Hope and Experience

Katy Samuels

> *If you have been called upon
> to travel the road
> described in these pages,
> then I dedicate this book to you.*

The front cover illustration is from an original oil painting entitled *Piedras Secas*, commissioned from Daniel Hyland, and used with permission.

© Katy Samuels 2014

Contents

Introduction 5

Chapter One	- No going back	8
Chapter Two	- In which a decision is made	13
Chapter Three	- Setting the scene	17
Chapter Four	- In which we assess skills - including our own	35
Chapter Five	- Which is dominated by questions	47

Stage Two

Chapter One	- The importance of folding and sorting	61
Chapter Two	- In which we face up to more problems	76
Chapter Three	- While the cat's away	84
Chapter Four	- Making sense of what we have	94

Stage Three

Chapter One	- Reviewing the situation	119
Chapter Two	- More of the same	132
Chapter Three	- A new year and a new set of challenges	140
Chapter Four	- A matter of some slight relief	152

Stage Four

Chapter One	- In which we search for signs of progress	163
Chapter Two	- Another flight from responsibility	174
Chapter Three	- Some successful problem solving	197
Chapter Four	- In conclusion	211

ORDER OUT OF CHAOS

Introduction

I had planned to call this book either *A Walk in the Wilderness* or *The Desert Road*. But, as I am hoping to arouse the interest of people who find themselves grappling with the demands of a loved one's dementia, such titles might sound somewhat negative. I have therefore looked at a quality which presented itself in our family situation - and took us all by surprise.

Creating order out of chaos is something most of us spend our lives trying to accomplish. The term does, however, take on a somewhat different meaning when used in the context of some neurological conditions. It is probably true to say that our brains are wired to achieve some measure of order within the chaos of ordinary daily living. This ordering may be in the workshop, the office, the garden - or even with the contents of the pocket, wallet, cutlery or sewing box! All areas will affect the quality and direction of our daily lives. The wiring can, however, take on a rather more dramatic nature when accompanying conditions such as dementia and autism.

But let me introduce you to the person most intimately concerned with walking this new road, and those family members who were in a position to share, in a limited way, the journey being undertaken.

Peter was born in 1934, educated in London and, on leaving school at eighteen years of age, spent three years at the Architectural College in London. It was a most splendid opportunity for him to continue to develop two of his four great passions. His first love, the design and beauty of cathedrals, parish churches and almost anything created from wood and stone, was linked to his second great love - Art and the History of Art. At the end of this course he was required to serve his two years National Service. During this time Peter realised that he needed to test what he felt was his calling to the priesthood. Consequently, at the age of twenty-three, he started a six year course at Kelham Theological College.

His ordination to the Anglican priesthood took place in St. Paul's Cathedral in London in 1962, and he was sent to his first curacy in Twickenham, Middlesex.

I am Katy. My background is in teaching. Peter and I met and were married in 1963 and lived in Middlesex until the birth of our first son, Paul, in 1964. After a second curacy in Rochester Diocese we moved to Lancashire, where, in 1967, our daughter Rachel was born.

Peter was now priest-in-charge of St. John's Church - where our third child, Mark, was born in 1969. In 1971 Peter was asked to be Rector of a church in the Manchester area. After eleven years at St. Andrew's Church he moved to a parish in Tameside, where he spent a further eleven years doing the work he had been called to do. Apart from his parochial ministry and watching his children develop and mature into young adults - of whom he was so proud - he continued to pursue, whenever time permitted, his great passions. I have already mentioned historic buildings and the appreciation of art, but the two remaining passions, which came into their own from 1971, were particularly satisfying as they were the results of his own creativity. Building, from scratch - without kits or preformed parts - a most faithful reconstruction of Bude Railway Station, complete with hand-made rolling stock, track, station buildings and surrounding landscape, was very demanding but intensely satisfying - particularly when his locomotive won the Bolton Trophy. Peter's life was always dominated by passions and it was to be no different when he moved into photography. His subjects were predominantly concerned with the history and architecture of ancient buildings. All this material would be carefully organised as the major part of his intended book on the re-ordering of the parish church in France.

In 1994 Peter resigned his Anglican Orders and, in 1995, was ordained as a priest in the Roman Catholic Church. He would serve, as curate, in the local Roman Catholic Church of St. Mary in Denton. He was very happy indeed in what he saw as a further development of his faith. Both Peter and I had some sort of re-thinking and reconstructing to do in our lives but everything seemed set fair for the years ahead. His book still hovered on the horizon - and it looked as though some text might eventually accompany the many pictures Peter had set on one side!

Grandchildren had started to arrive:
Paul has Danny and Alex; Rachel has Joe and Amber;
Mark has Molly and William.

But to return to Peter. The re-ordering would not be of any parish church in France, but, most cruelly, the destruction of a shy and unassuming person, a man of considerable intellect who was happiest when surrounded by, and immersed in, his beloved books.

On careful and honest reflection I can say that there had been mild signs of memory loss from the early nineties, but, as in most of life, excuses can be quickly made for any slight deviations from what one might have regarded as the norm.

Chapter One - In which the scene is set

"Katy, I'm lost . . ." When Peter said this we were approaching a well-signposted roundabout we had negotiated several hundred times before. It was July 8th in the year 2000 and Peter's words caused a definite ringing of alarm bells in my brain. We had been on a morning visit to Bolsover Castle in Derbyshire and were returning home, on the main A623 Chesterfield/Manchester Road. I was driving, after a most interesting and enjoyable morning, during which Peter had appeared to be absorbed in the structural changes that had been made in the castle. I pointed out that we were approaching a roundabout, which would show that we were on the right road to Manchester. Peter then said, "No, I mean I am lost in my head." This would be an expression he would use on many future occasions - and was the remark which would cause such devastation in all our lives. When Peter continued to express concerns over different problems he was encountering we decided that a visit to the GP might be appropriate. He referred Peter to the local hospital and an appointment was made to see one of the consultant psychiatrists.

It may be an idea to use Peter's own words to describe his condition. He dictated the following letter, addressed to the psychiatrist, because, as he put it, he was unable to think and talk, or think and write at the same time.

> "I have been experiencing a significant level of memory loss, which has been increasing over the last few months. I have been seeing my GP for several years now with annoying symptoms of depression, including memory loss, and am currently taking Dothiepin capsules to help control some of the anxiety and panic attacks I have been

experiencing. However, as my memory loss is interfering with all aspects of my life, I asked my GP if there was anything that could be done to slow down the pace of loss. He advised me that he was not able to prescribe any of the possible drugs, as that was in the hands of psychiatrists. So I am here to ask you if you can help me.

"What is happening to my memory? Although I am able to remember details of learning, information and experiences I have collected over the last sixty years, when it comes to what was said ten or fifteen minutes ago then I am starting to struggle.

"I am also having difficulty in making sense of some of the things that are said to me. By that I mean that I find it very difficult to sort out conversations unless they are conducted slowly. I frequently lose track of what is being said.

"I have to keep looking in my diary to find out which day of the week we are at, and checking up on what I am supposed to be doing and where I am supposed to be.

"It is very difficult to learn new skills because I cannot remember the sequences involved. An example is my acquisition of *Paint Shop* for the computer - I cannot understand it because I cannot follow the sequences involved. Although, in 1988, I bought myself a computer and worked out, quite independently of anybody else, exactly how to use it, I am now reduced to spending three or four days writing out my sermons at the rate of about one word a minute and spending a lot of time staring at the screen. This is not an ideal way to work.

"My impaired hearing does not help. I do have a very

> satisfactory hearing aid - the Hidden Hearing variety - but that does not help me to make sense of what is being said."

This was the last coherent letter he was able to dictate and, consequently, later reports to the doctor were not his own. The words were not his and may or may not have said what he really wanted to say. I must note that, without exception, we have experienced only kindliness, respect, patience and compassionate professionalism from each of the three psychiatrists we have met with over these last ten years.

Peter was prescribed a therapeutic dose of Exelon and was tolerating the medication very well. By this time he was serving as curate in our local Catholic church, but it was becoming increasingly difficult to mask the problems arising from the memory loss. He could still drive his car and carry out his pastoral duties but, slowly and almost imperceptibly, the signs of the huge struggle were leaving their mark. By July 2004, he was significantly impaired by the accumulation of problems. He could no longer drive and had to accept the appalling reality of having to sign a letter of resignation to his bishop. I found writing the letter for him a very painful experience because, once again, his decision had, of necessity, been influenced by others.

In one report to the psychiatrist, in 2004, I found myself writing the following note:

> "It is evident that, frequently, Peter does not understand what is being said to him. Neither does he understand what he is reading - he has been on page 57 of his library book for the last nine weeks, even though he picks it up and looks at it on a very regular - almost hourly - basis. He reads *The Times* each day but does not remember reading it. Unless I move the paper out of the Study at the end of the day he will read

> Monday's paper on Tuesday, Wednesday, Thursday or Friday as though it is the new paper."

And so he struggled on through the next three years becoming more and more suicidal, frustrated, aggressive, depressed and eventually lacking in motivation.

By the middle of June 2007, and having benefited from some additional medication, there is a rather different character emerging. He has withdrawn a long way into - or away from - himself. The suicidal outbursts have gone, as has the person who once was Peter. I have the shell to care for but that keen intellect has gone away. He does not recognize our house as his home, neither does he know that I am his wife. In fact, on one occasion he asked me who I was and, when I mentioned that I was his wife, he replied, 'I have no wife.' There is not a great deal one can say or do in the face of such a positive declaration of fact. Except, of course, to keep going. Wife or not, he does seem to know that he is safe in the house and that I am the person who looks after him. For that small mercy - and the fact that he is still continent - we must be thankful.

Another fact that has been concealed over these many years is Peter's autism.

Odd behaviour can be dealt with, but real obsessions are a little more of a problem - Alzheimer's disease and Asperger's Syndrome make strange bedfellows. By June 2007, Peter's condition was reasonably stable - perhaps a little more confused and a little less co-ordinated, but definitely more peaceful and content. I had not been able to take Peter to church for some while, because he resisted being 'organized' by someone else as far as dressing and preparing to leave the house was concerned. There is, as we well know, only so much pressure one can put on another human being before the situation becomes intolerable. That situation, in many cases, could lead to signs of aggression - which no one would want.

A turning point came on October 9th 2007 when Peter was due to see the psychiatrist at the hospital. This proved to be impossible, because of four days of extraordinary behaviour when Peter was unable to understand or co-operate with anything. He was not able to allow himself to be parted from his clothes in order to have a bath. In fact he could not be parted from his chair. He ended up staying in the same clothes for no less than four days - and nights. As we could not keep the appointment, the psychiatrist came out to see Peter at home. He then suggested involving the community psychiatric nurse, with a view to considering whether or not there might be some appropriate involvement or even intervention. It was at this point that I took that proverbial look into the future - or was it the abyss? The brain does inexplicable things at times. In my case, and on this occasion, there seemed to be a choice between two challenging options - with no certainty of success, whichever one was chosen. One thing was very evident. Whichever course of action was taken would need to be taken with a willingness to reckon on the absurdity of life in all situations. Of course, there was nothing clever or exceptional in considering the options. Life has the same options for every situation. The first option is to keep going. The second option is to cave in. There it is. It is as simple as that . . . Keep Going. Cave In. Which will it be?

Chapter Two - In which a decision is made - with an essential chain reaction

I suppose that, after fifteen years of niggles and eight years of Alzheimer's cruelty, I had found very little information on understanding and managing the disease in a domestic set-up. But that is what thousands of people - we call them carers - are struggling, each day, to do, as they give of their very best to care for a loved one suffering from Alzheimer's disease.

As we know, this is a disease in which the number of nerve cells in the brain - called neurons - gradually reduces and this causes the brain to shrink. These neurons are irreplaceable and, as more and more cells are destroyed, so the disease becomes progressively worse. The nerve cells are absolutely essential for any activity involving language and problem solving. They are needed for instructing muscles how and when to work, so that, without them, there is going to be a problem. Experts will tell us that each neuron is equipped with an axon and a dendrite, which will be closely involved in the passing of a nervous impulse from one to the other, via a space called the synapse. We can sympathize with the fate of the synapse and the intricate collapse of these neuron cells, but it is the *carer* who has to cope with the realities of these intricacies.

It was this that led me to think that it would be worth charting what was happening in our family, and perhaps share some of the information. It seemed to me that keeping some sort of record would be a manageable and useful means of dealing with both the developing situation and any information which might come our way. After two years of reporting - and keeping going - I felt that I wanted to share this anecdotal research with people who might have rather different connections with Alzheimer's. People who might be asking themselves the question, 'How possible is it to maintain an acceptable quality of life for someone with Alzheimer's disease, from whom the ability to control or contribute to his or her quality of life has been removed? How *do-able* is the enterprise?'

This book, *Order out of Chaos*, is really a compilation of some significant, and possibly relevant, extracts from the seven hundred and thirty-one daily entries (2008 was a leap year!) in the journals I have maintained over the two year period between November 2007 and November 2009. Because they are extracts, some entries will refer to events which will have been recorded in the daily entries, but which may not appear in this work. My apologies if you find this confusing.

If you have read thus far - and are still interested - I would like to think that you too might feel like undertaking a somewhat daunting task, and have a real go at Keeping Going with your own situation. The most important factor to keep in mind is that *you* are as individual and unique as the person for whom you are caring - in whatever capacity, be it family, domestic or professional.

Friday November 2nd 2007

Today is the day I have started to plan the form the record will take. Debi is the community psychiatric nurse assigned to Peter, and I intend involving her in the recording process in whatever way seems appropriate. Some professional input will be of considerable value when trying to assess and monitor the progression of the illness. An essential ingredient in the whole process will be the support of Paul, Rachel and Mark - and the beautiful and wonderful grandchildren who are part of our daily life. Their presence will provide every reason for what I have to describe as Keeping Going. So, we are now ready to begin.

The plan is to keep a daily journal of events during the day, which seem worthy of comment - should any arise. Failing that, I will record the mundane. After four weeks, Debi and I will discuss the contents of the journal, and consider any implications for either or any of us. It also seems a helpful idea to rank the day, not according to Peter's behaviour, because that would be most unfair, but according to the quality of the day. This would include whatever was good for Peter, for me and for the grandchildren who, as I have already mentioned, form such an important, joyful and essential part of our daily lives. The ranking would be a simple scale of 1-10 with 10 being very good and 1 being not very good at all! This might be used as a cross reference when looking for a possible pattern in behaviour. It might also suggest whether or not different strategies may or may not be working effectively. My hope is that it will be constructive rather than destructive.

Perhaps I should mention, at this stage, that I do keep both the front and the back doors locked, with the keys well out of sight. This helps all of us because, until I started locking the doors, Peter would be wandering round the garden, even weeing in the garden and then trying to escape onto the road and pavement. *Inappropriate Urination* might have been the title of a cleverly written book but, as it is not well tolerated in the residential areas of the UK, I have made it my responsibility to prevent at least one person from indulging in such excessive behaviour. This does not stop him from trying to open the doors, but he gives up all hope when the doors resist. Locking the doors and making sure that there is no form of heating which can be tampered with, turned on or switched off, does mean that I can, and do, leave Peter on his own while I go out. The times are restricted to the time he is in bed - which is a lot of the time - and the time he is sitting in the Study. The electric kettle and microwave are always switched off at the wall and there is no other form of heating apart from the radiators. This has been a deliberate arrangement to ensure as safe an environment as possible. As with children, there are no matches or candles within reach or sight. But, to return to recording and ranking. It seems appropriate to use the journal itself to describe what might seem to be relevant events - and perhaps that will be sufficient to suggest the reasoning behind the ranking.

Another very important development has been the purchasing of an exercise bike. I woke up one morning, thinking that I was twenty years old and out riding my bicycle. Following an impulse I went to one of the Retail Stores and found, listed in the catalogue, a splendidly simple exercise bike for forty nine pounds and ninety nine pence. I bought the machine and hurried home to try and assemble the parts and create a whole bike. This took rather more time than the manufacturer had imagined but, eventually, I was able to place the newly assembled bicycle in the room which had once been Peter's photography dark room. It had been re-ordered as a very pleasant workroom, with some of Peter's award-winning large sized photographs displayed on the walls. These were especially chosen to enhance the cycling! So, armed with an atlas and surrounded by pictures, I can begin a tour of the world, which will now be my oyster! Who can want for anything more, I ask myself - but fail to give an answer.

How odd it seems to be preparing to turn the spotlight on the daily life of a very shy man, who did his utmost to avoid being the centre of attention at any time in his life. Wearing a cassock and a clerical collar provided him with a form of camouflage, which then allowed him to function, with great sensitivity, as a priest, and yet allowed the man behind the camouflage to remain hidden. But the person who once was Peter, with his keen intellect and very droll sense of humour has gone - although not completely. One day, from a deeply withdrawn state, with what appeared to be full recognition and, with a gentle smile, he said his familiar "Ahh mmmm" before lapsing back into his withdrawn world.

Chapter Three - Setting the scene

The scene has been set and the characters, in order of appearance, are ready to make their respective entrances, so the curtain can now be raised - and the play can begin . . !

Wednesday November 8th 2007

Today has not been a good day at all. The main reason has been the way Peter has felt the need to shadow my every move, and tidy up the equipment I have been using - for cooking, cleaning and even when sorting the music for Sunday. Creating order has been very high on his agenda. The wandering has lasted over two hours. He really ought to know every nook and cranny in this house, but, of course, that is not quite how it works. Having a bath was not a problem tonight, although he got in and out of bed no less than five times - to check on what I was doing in the next room. I was riding my sanity-saving exercise bicycle. There was one odd little event at bath time tonight. I was starting to wash Peter's hair when he suddenly took exception to the water coming out of the hose and became agitated. I gave him a small towel to hold over his face. This he took and proceeded to tie it round his head - rather like a bandanna. Needless to say it had to be removed in order for his hair to be washed. But, it was a good bid for freedom, if not independence. A ranking of 6/10 would seem reasonable.

Thursday November 9th 2007

Today has been a very good day. While I went to Amber's school assembly, Peter had lined up a whole box of cutlery, four tea towels, three cups and saucers, two cereal bowls and two copies of *The Times*. He is really pleased with his work and took great pleasure in showing me the arrangement in the kitchen. I told him it was excellent work and he looked very pleased. I am planning a trip to Birmingham on Saturday, so I shall not hurry Peter to bed tomorrow. The plan would be that I would leave here at 7 o'clock on Saturday morning, collect Amber and drive down to Bournville to see Paul, his wife Muna, Danny (11) and Alex (8). We would arrive at the swimming baths, at 9.30 am, watch the children swim and then go home with them by 11.30 am. It would then be time to return to Manchester. A short visit, but a very important and valuable visit. This is a simple demonstration of how important the family circle is in Keeping Going. Valuing each other's strengths is not only appropriate but is also vital for survival. Peter was bathed and in bed by 12.35 am. He went to sleep quickly and I will rank the day at 8/10.

Saturday November 11th 2007

A good day generally - apart from a blip this evening. It was, however, a most useful blip because I learnt a very important fact, which could be of great help in the future - provided I remember to put the learning into practice. There is usually a period of marching, or wandering, all over the house at about half past six in the evening. These wanderings can last up to an hour, or even longer. I suspect, now, that what is happening is that Peter is doing an inventory of the house and its contents - both human and non-human. If I am working around the house then he finds the wandering process most confusing. As often as he returns to wherever I am working, he then seems to have to start all over again. Today I have been forced - by circumstances - to stay sitting in the study, in a chair and occupying myself with something quiet and harmless - such as working on the big tapestry. If I stay in the same place, doing the same thing, then Peter can go through his inventory in half the time it would otherwise take. Once he is certain that no other person is in the house, and that he has lined up enough objects, then, and only then, can he allow himself to sit down and spend time looking at his books. The cutlery has been lined up again - all in order of size and function. Today merits 8/10 - mainly because of what I have learned.

Questions for the experts.

Is obsessive and repetitive behaviour, such as I am seeing, typical of dementia in general?

If it is not necessarily typical, and there has been strong evidence that a lot of autistic behaviour has been modified or, most likely, suppressed, over a professional working life, then might we expect to see a reverting to the obsessive rituals which may have featured in early childhood?

Bearing in mind that autism would not have been recognised or understood during Peter's childhood, signs of bizarre and odd behaviour would have been regarded unfavourably. Any correction, or even punishment, might possibly, then, have been a process of working <u>against</u> the child's nature rather than <u>with</u> the child's nature?

Is there any thinking at all about a link between autism in the young child and dementia at the other end of the age range? There must be a great deal of anecdotal material which could help to shed some light on the problem!

Thursday November 16th 2007

Debi arrived, as previously arranged, and we spent some time in going over the behaviour and achievements of the last two weeks. Several interesting points have emerged as a result of our discussions. Debi is of the opinion that Peter is showing signs of Sundowning. I have looked this up on the internet, but I have to say that it is nowhere near as promising or exciting as it sounds. It seems that, with the going down of the sun, people with various forms of dementia display patterns of restlessness, agitation and, with some, periods of business - pronounced *busy-ness*. Peter appears to fit into some of these slots, so perhaps this is a new string to his bow. Debi has also suggested that, instead of giving a single dose of tranquillising Promazine at breakfast time - whenever that happens to be - we give him a double dose at teatime - when the sun goes down - and continue with the double dose at bedtime - whenever that happens to be. This has been Day One of the new order. I will continue this pattern for two weeks, unless anything untoward presents itself. The day itself ranks as 5/10 - largely due to restlessness. Cycling is called for.

My daily task is to cycle for seven miles each day and, should the fancy take me, to remind myself of some of the wonderful places Peter and I have visited over these many years. Tonight I opened the atlas at a page devoted to Jerusalem. Peter and I stayed in Jerusalem for three nights, during our pilgrimage to the Holy Land in October 1995. This visit was the realisation of a dream we had shared over many years. With this thought in mind I mounted my trusty steed and set off for the Holy Land.

Before long I found myself standing, with Peter, in a veritable labyrinth of narrow lanes and tiny dwellings. We were in the Arab enclave adjoining the Dome of the Rock, which is the most exquisite and glorious of Muslim shrines. We were hoping to find the way into St. Anne's Church. Although we did not succeed in finding the way in we found ourselves at the beginning of what was to be a fascinating and, at times, disturbing experience. I suspect that, at this stage, we must have fitted the description of Innocents Abroad quite easily. Armed with the map, Peter led the way forward. Access to a map in no way ensures progress with me, so I did what I always did in that sort of situation - followed. We seemed to be walking along some exceedingly congested streets with a lot of pedestrians for company. Quite suddenly we took a side lane, which transported us, in only a few minutes, to a completely different world.

This was a world of silence. Of walls, of graffiti, of sudden bends and sharp corners. Not only had the environment changed but the light had also started to change as the sky became darker. We realised that, here in the Holy Land, there would not be that period of dusk which we experience in England. When darkness came it would come very quickly and, although we were the proud possessors of a map, we still had very little idea of where we were in this labyrinth, or even where we were hoping to be. As we walked along these alleys we were rather quiet. Neither of us wished to express concern by voicing any sort of anxiety. We were, however, both more than a little worried by now. But, as the night sky started to take possession of the light, we had the blessed relief of stumbling, quite literally, on what passed for a main road. Now we might be able to make some sort of sense of the map. Well, one of us might. Before very long we found one of the main gates of Jerusalem - Herod's Gate - and breathed a sigh of relief, as we believed it would be plain sailing - or walking - from then on. We walked quickly and confidently through Herod's Gate and found ourselves in the modern part of the Arab city. But we were actually walking into another trap. We had the map but nothing looked the same in the darkness. Up and down, backwards and forwards we walked, again trying to stifle our own inward fears. Then, at last, the light shone in our darkness, as we happened to come across the Travel Agency owned by the wonderful Guide of our Pilgrimage Group. We breathed a sigh of relief and went to inquire the whereabouts of our Hotel. Within five minutes we were back in the safety of the Meridian Hotel and preparing to collect our key. Feeling extremely thankful that we were in one piece, unmugged, unrobbed and still on holiday, I did nevertheless, find myself thinking the unthinkable. Whereas I could very easily lose myself, with or without a map, how on earth had Peter, who had the eye of a hawk and the homing instinct of a professional homing pigeon, managed to acquire this new skill of being lost while in possession of a map. Needless to say there was a very simple answer. We had not been lost at all. How foolish of me. I should have known better. Perhaps, next time, I will be in possession of the map and lose us both successfully...

I have returned to Denton, but, rest assured, I shall return to Jerusalem before too long.

Thursday November 22nd 2007

Although recording takes place on a daily basis it is often very revealing to see, on looking back, how a change in behaviour - which appears suddenly to have taken place - has really been slowly emerging during the days or weeks before. Such signs are not always easy to pick up, but any detail of change - should one have the time to notice it - could well be a sign of things to come. This next note shows how one skill appeared in a polished state, without the early stages having been noticed.

The day started uneventfully enough at 10.25 am, although this was far, far, too early. The consequence has been almost non-stop walking from room to room, turning light switches in all directions, and, a great deal of lining up. Peter has been trying to wear his hat for most of the day. He has, most successfully, tidied up the wicker basket in which he seems to have decided that he is supposed to keep his paper, books currently in use and any other important-looking piece of paper. I have never known Peter tidy anything before, so I have been most impressed with this newly revealed skill. Everything has been arranged according to size and the capacious basket looks well-filled. I am really impressed. However, the walking has persisted well into the evening, finally subsiding some time after nine o'clock. Mercifully he has been sitting down in his chair for the best part of an hour, so perhaps we can both unwind a little. The constant clicking of light switches can quickly assume the qualities of the so-called Water Torture. It is almost half past midnight and Peter is in the bath, with tooth cleaning to follow.

Rachel has had a positive brainwave over the toothbrush, which I have followed to good effect. The idea is to squash the paste into the brush, so that it does not fall off during the somewhat fraught journey to the mouth. It seems very successful. The day however is really only worth 2/10.

Thursday November 29th 2007

Neither William (5), nor Joe (15), has been well enough to attend school today, so we have enjoyed a happy day together at home. Peter has been restless since he got up at 12.30 pm. He has shadowed me constantly and has been rather hard work. The truth of the matter is that his behaviour is so much like a toddler's behaviour that it can, at times, seem somewhat draining. A toddler, behaving like a toddler, does not have the same effect of course. A toddler's behaviour is appropriate to the age; Peter's behaviour is not age appropriate and so is much, much, more stressful. It is now after just midnight and time to start the bath and bed process. The day ranked as 3/10 until the latter part of the evening - at which point it shot up to 6/10.

Sunday December 2nd 2007

Today has been a good day, despite the rain. Again there has been a lot of wandering about and sorting things out. Today Peter's attention has concentrated itself on the music on top of the piano. Tonight we have had a lot of switch clicking - always connected to Peter's insatiable need to check rooms, baskets, drawers and other such exciting places.

Nevertheless, as days go, today is on a par with yesterday, so, unless everything falls apart at bedtime - whenever that is - the day should be worth 8/10. Of course, if he attempts to open the front door one more time. . . the score might be a little different. Challenging the door is a little bit of a pain at times because, although the outer door is locked, he still has the chance to fiddle with the chain, fiddle with the little catch on the inner door and then rattle the outer door. He loves these attempted bids for freedom, so I must be very mean to keep putting obstacles in the way.

It is now 2.45 am and the best-laid plans of mice and men have been well and truly scuppered - to mix the metaphors! As the once hot bath is now very tepid I shall get in the bath and then go to bed. Peter has suddenly discovered not only a great deal of energy but also some frenetic cerebral activity. He has been talking non-stop about three large books he has taken from the book-case and is, currently, busy removing some of the 4000 - yes, four thousand - transparencies from the files. These transparencies have all been carefully documented from the days he was able to practise his great hobby of photography, and will contain many essential pictures for the Book that will not now be written. As this is the only really comprehensive piece of filing and ordering he has ever accomplished, I find myself dreading the thought of getting them all back into their rightful files and places. On the other hand, I ask myself, will it really matter? I have taken the light bulb out of the bedroom, so that when Peter does come up to bed I shall only have to hear the clicking of the switch. There will be no violent illuminating of the bedroom. I have another plan for tomorrow. The day ends with 0/10 - but remember the good part. It could so easily have been 8/10.

Monday December 3rd 2007

This is my plan. Regardless of protest, Peter will get up at 11 o'clock - not a minute later. During the day he will take a walk round the park

- regardless of the weather, although if it is wet we will walk along the road. He will be heavily involved in light housework, including a lot of washing-up and will be glad to get into bed before midnight.

It is now 11.45am and I have dragged Peter from his bed for the fourth time. He must be tired but that is no reason for changing the plan. He keeps trying to get back into bed - even though I keep stripping the bed. This is clear evidence of cerebral activity. He closes his eyes so that I will think he's asleep. An old trick which is doomed to failure. He is now fully dressed and ready to face the world - and a day's work. There is also the arrival of Cousin John to consider.

It is now 11.00pm and Peter is about to get into the bath. Has the new plan worked? Time alone will tell. If the time is *pm* then the plan has worked. If it has got to *am,* then the plan requires a little more thought. The day deserves 9/10.

Tuesday December 4th 2007

What an achievement! The thought of 11/10 springs into my mind. Following the new pattern, I stand over Peter until he manages to dress and can prepare to come down for breakfast. I called him at 11 o'clock and he has managed to be downstairs by 12 o'clock. I do realise that, for the most part, the idea of sequencing is now a very rarely practised skill, but, if he is supervised, then he can make progress. It is when I give him his freedom that the problems arise. However, the day has passed in a very satisfactory way. Peter has done a lot of lining up, walking about, washing up and has even tried to respond to John's carefully articulated and complex questioning on matters concerning the times they shared as boys in Croydon. It would be so interesting to know something of what Peter makes of all this. He asked me again who I was - and seemed content to know that I was the person who looked after him and that there was nothing to be frightened about.

Peter had a bath and was in bed by 12.10 am - which is a most acceptable time, especially as he has not felt the need to wander round the house and turn on the light in John's room in the middle of the night. All in all, it has been a very good day.

Friday December 14th 2007

Today has been a total contrast to yesterday. Peter has followed me around constantly and has been putting on his coat and hat at every possible opportunity. He does not appear to want to go out, simply to wear his outdoor clothes. The house is not cold, neither is the man. He is just very restless. I am hoping for a calm day and evening as Molly and William are coming to stay until Saturday evening. So far the day is only 3/10 but if he lasts the night without disturbing the children I shall give the day a large bonus. Therefore I shall reserve my judgement until Saturday evening. One must always be fair.

Sunday December 17th 2007

Tonight we shall attend Brian Basan's pre-Christmas soiree. So anything could happen as far as Peter is concerned. Will he manage the occasion or shall we have to leave early and walk home? We ended up going by car as the weather became very frosty and I did not think Peter would be able to walk there - and back. As it turned out we had to leave the party immediately after dinner, as Peter was oblivious to his surroundings, unaware of anybody else in the room and just wanting to wander round and tidy and re-order somebody else's possessions. Naturally, I could not allow such behaviour to go unchecked, so we left. What else could one do? Bath time and bedtime followed the usual - and now rather tedious - pattern and eventually Peter got into bed soon after 1.30 am. So much for the soporific effects of two large glasses of red wine, two ladles of

Promazine and one Zopiclone tablet. I do sometimes wonder exactly what goes into a lethal cocktail.

Tuesday January 1st 2008

Peter got up at 3.00 pm and had a very good day indeed - until bedtime. So, without more ado, I shall rank the day as 9/10 - because I was able to celebrate the New Year by cleaning the house. This may not sound much of an achievement but, to me, it proved to be a very calming and satisfying activity. It could easily count as respite! So, when Peter did get up, life could proceed in a more positive way.

The whole process at bedtime is still a puzzle to me. I go upstairs at bedtime and turn back the duvet, so that the room looks exactly like a bedroom with a bed ready for somebody to get into. I run the bath and leave the clean pyjamas hanging on the bathroom door handle. These routines have been followed in exactly this way for the last forty years, so should be part of what happens at the end of the day. Now, why should Peter take off his jacket, hang it on the banisters - or any other unlikely place - before trying to remake the bed and then walking round looking totally vacant? What follows is now very predictable! I suggest that he might get undressed ready to get into the bath. He looks at me without comprehension and picks up the nearest object. It is only when I firmly escort him into the bathroom and insist that he take off his shoes, trousers and jersey - one command at a time - that we can make any progress. Remember, I am supposed to be riding my bicycle. The one I bought from Argos to help control selfish and stress-inducing feelings. The theory is excellent - the reality, perhaps, not quite so certain. I think I have almost reached Poland - and while I am issuing commands I am not reducing the famous stress levels. Sometimes I can feel the laughter rising in my throat - I suppose some might describe this as hysteria - and have to turn away in case Peter thinks I am laughing at him. That would be most unkind. Once his realised that the only thing that galvanises him into action - such as trying to take off his shoes - is if I raise my voice very slightly and issue a command in a clear firm voice. I am not talking about shouting, but I am talking about a determined 'I am in control and you will please do as I ask you,' voice. This is not what you want in a caring situation but, sometimes, it seems to be the only catalyst to trigger off the necessary reaction. The ending to the day was reasonable enough, except that I am left thinking and feeling things I would prefer not to think and feel. Perhaps the day should be ranked as 8/10 because it has turned up a few different ideas.

This may be an appropriate point at which to mention the very mixed feelings we may experience at any time during the day. One aspect has worried me in that I can see that, considering I am trying to write about Peter, almost everything I write is linked to me, my thoughts and my preferences. Of course the absence of any normal dialogue in a home will create an odd situation. But I have realized that it is not a wrong or bad thing to make certain that the carer's needs, real or imagined, have a rightful and possibly prominent place in each and every day. If the carer is able to feel that domestic harmony does not depend on *excessive* self-sacrifice then the situation is probably being well managed. Perhaps it is not too unreasonable to hope for some element of shared responsibility between the carer and the one being cared for. This may not be as paradoxical as it may sound. I suspect I shall have to return to that thought in a few months' time.

Sunday February 3rd 2008

Today has been another interesting day, influenced partly by a re-thinking on my part of our current situation. I am increasingly conscious of the very wide range of views and attitudes which have some bearing on the way carers - and those for whom they care - carry out their differing responsibilities. That may sound odd, but it seems

Promazine and one Zopiclone tablet. I do sometimes wonder exactly what goes into a lethal cocktail.

Tuesday January 1st 2008

Peter got up at 3.00 pm and had a very good day indeed - until bedtime. So, without more ado, I shall rank the day as 9/10 - because I was able to celebrate the New Year by cleaning the house. This may not sound much of an achievement but, to me, it proved to be a very calming and satisfying activity. It could easily count as respite! So, when Peter did get up, life could proceed in a more positive way.

The whole process at bedtime is still a puzzle to me. I go upstairs at bedtime and turn back the duvet, so that the room looks exactly like a bedroom with a bed ready for somebody to get into. I run the bath and leave the clean pyjamas hanging on the bathroom door handle. These routines have been followed in exactly this way for the last forty years, so should be part of what happens at the end of the day. Now, why should Peter take off his jacket, hang it on the banisters - or any other unlikely place - before trying to remake the bed and then walking round looking totally vacant? What follows is now very predictable! I suggest that he might get undressed ready to get into the bath. He looks at me without comprehension and picks up the nearest object. It is only when I firmly escort him into the bathroom and insist that he take off his shoes, trousers and jersey - one command at a time - that we can make any progress. Remember, I am supposed to be riding my bicycle. The one I bought from Argos to help control selfish and stress-inducing feelings. The theory is excellent - the reality, perhaps, not quite so certain. I think I have almost reached Poland - and while I am issuing commands I am not reducing the famous stress levels. Sometimes I can feel the laughter rising in my throat - I suppose some might describe this as hysteria - and have to turn away in case Peter thinks I am laughing at him. That would be most unkind. Once his clothes have found their way into the laundry basket the next challenge presents itself. Namely, where is the bath? Well, of course, he is standing next to the bath - which is half-full of water, originally hot and bubbly, but now tepid. The big question now is how to get into the bath. Once this has been achieved then he can wash himself. Sequencing. That is what is missing. You may be able to order, but can you sequence?

Sunday January 6th 2008

The day has been unsurpassed for restlessness, wandering and foolishness. I would like to dignify the behaviour by using a different word but I cannot find one in my vocabulary. So I shall have to settle for a day ranked at 4/10.

Monday January 7th 2008

I have realised that a pattern seems to be emerging in respect of some of Peter's behaviour. He is showing further signs of regression as far as his understanding of language is concerned. More worrying is *my* continued regression in understanding his language. I shall have to sort out exactly what I think I am seeing in the pattern of his behaviour. It definitely involves his need to possess everything I am holding or even looking at. He seems to think all those items belong to him and, therefore, he must, at all costs, gain their possession.

Tuesday January 8th 2008

This becomes more and more interesting - or more and more frustrating, depending on your involvement. Peter got up just before 1.30 pm and dressed reasonably well, including attempting to put on his tie. He then sat in the Study with his book until it was time for me to go to Marple Bridge for William and Molly. I made him a cup of coffee and gave him a piece of chocolate muffin - he is losing weight, hence the unusual indulgence. On my return he was still sitting down and there was no evidence of any tidying up or rearranging activity and I had the impression that he had indeed spent the one and a half hours sitting - perhaps in silent contemplation. It then became time to return the children to Marple Bridge and to collect Joe and Amber from their post-school activities. When, at six o'clock, we had all arrived back home, including Rachel, Peter emerged from the Study and decided to stand in the small space between the kitchen and the family room. It was Rachel who noticed that Peter was then standing perfectly still and appearing to register nothing. He stared into space for perhaps half a minute, patted the top of his head and then tried to measure his height against Joe's. (This is something he now does fairly frequently and becomes very excited by the result.) When Stephen, who is over six feet tall, came into the room, Peter became very excited and positively leapt into the air. Never in my life have I seen Peter jump. This jump was an astounding jump. A High Jump in the true sense of the word. However he did not need to jump with Joe. . !

Eating his dinner was a small challenge but that was because he had to keep checking that the dinner in front of him was for him to eat. The drying of the crockery and cutlery took a long time because he had to find a different resting place for every single item. Having accomplished this he went into the Study and sat in the chair. I took in the coffee and said I was just going to Choir Practice and would be coming back very soon. He nodded wisely and made no attempt to follow me to the front door. Again, when I returned he was still sitting in the Study, still staring at his book and appeared to be completely calm - or vacant. I do not think there is any difference in Peter's concept of the passage of time between five minutes and two hours. Now the rest of the evening was quiet and uneventful - until bedtime. I have noticed, over the last three weeks that Peter is not responding to any of my prompts as far as the getting ready for bath and bed rituals are concerned. To my great disappointment I have realised that the only thing that galvanises him into action - such as trying to take off his shoes - is if I raise my voice very slightly and issue a command in a clear firm voice. I am not talking about shouting, but I am talking about a determined 'I am in control and you will please do as I ask you,' voice. This is not what you want in a caring situation but, sometimes, it seems to be the only catalyst to trigger off the necessary reaction. The ending to the day was reasonable enough, except that I am left thinking and feeling things I would prefer not to think and feel. Perhaps the day should be ranked as 8/10 because it has turned up a few different ideas.

This may be an appropriate point at which to mention the very mixed feelings we may experience at any time during the day. One aspect has worried me in that I can see that, considering I am trying to write about Peter, almost everything I write is linked to me, my thoughts and my preferences. Of course the absence of any normal dialogue in a home will create an odd situation. But I have realized that it is not a wrong or bad thing to make certain that the carer's needs, real or imagined, have a rightful and possibly prominent place in each and every day. If the carer is able to feel that domestic harmony does not depend on *excessive* self-sacrifice then the situation is probably being well managed. Perhaps it is not too unreasonable to hope for some element of shared responsibility between the carer and the one being cared for. This may not be as paradoxical as it may sound. I suspect I shall have to return to that thought in a few months' time.

Sunday February 3rd 2008

Today has been another interesting day, influenced partly by a re-thinking on my part of our current situation. I am increasingly conscious of the very wide range of views and attitudes which have some bearing on the way carers - and those for whom they care - carry out their differing responsibilities. That may sound odd, but it seems to me that those being cared-for may also have built-in responsibilities to which they make an automatic and unconscious response. So, in our own situation, I have realised that I have been looking at Peter and the life he is living now, as though he is still the person he used to be - before dementia took control of areas of his brain. If I regard Peter in this way then I cannot reconcile the way he has to live with the person he used to be. The whole situation becomes unacceptable and grotesque. But, if I look carefully at the person Peter has become - with his rapidly shrinking world and his increasing loss of skills and understanding - then I see that the way he is living his life takes on a new quality. I can see that, with all those considerations, his quality of life is very good indeed. If one lists the positive aspects, such as there being no more fear, no obvious frustration, no apparent worries or even a realisation that anything has been lost in his life, join those ideas with the comfort of a warm pleasant home, nourishing food and plenty of coffee, clean clothes, polished shoes, his library of books and a very comfortable bed, then life seems to have plenty of positive aspects. He sleeps for at least twelve hours a day - which reduces the opportunities for stress and distress - and looks the picture of frail good health! I can see that, if I judge the quality of his life by these standards, I have some reasonable idea as to how to continue making things work properly. I suspect I have been somewhat slow in reaching this level of understanding, but it would seem to me that it should be easier to carry on with the caring job if one has a realistic understanding of the current situation - and a willingness to notice and respond to any changes in the situation. I hope this is as easy to do as it is to say. The day deserves at least 10/10 - because I have learnt a lot from it!

Friday February 15th 2008

I took the children out and left Peter sleeping. He was still sleeping when we returned at 1.45 pm. The day was busy but he did get up eventually. I soon discovered that he could not understand anything about taking off his clothes and dressing. I ended up putting on most of his clothes. This is not because he is physically unable to use his hands, but because he cannot understand the processes required. Eating has been another problem. He has not seemed to register that the food in front of him is for him to eat. Although, after he had cleaned his teeth, I gave him some mouth wash - which he swallowed as soon as I turned my back to pick up a towel from the floor. I gave him some more, had some myself and we stood there looking at each other, making fish-like faces for the required 30 seconds. How daft is that. . ! Daft it may be, but the mission was accomplished. He tried to count the children today, which is surely worth a ranking of 10/10.

I do not think I have mentioned that I have put Peter's hat and coat away. He has been putting them on and sitting in the chair. He then refuses to take them off, so they are better off in the wardrobe - where he would never dream of looking for any item of clothing.

I am still trying to work out why Peter cannot hear what I am saying and yet can hear the initial sound of an incoming telephone call! He cannot hear the television and yet he can hear the sound of a car going past the house. If I stifle a cough, or even if I cough, he asks me what I have said. If I call his name he does not hear: if I call the name of anybody else he answers fairly quickly.

There may be a link between the times when Peter feels unable to have a bath and to go to bed, and the decrease in his intellectual functioning. I do note that he has deteriorated, quite noticeably, on the days following the times he has not managed to go up to bed to go to sleep. Why? As Peter's world shrinks, I wonder if he is cancelling out things that he may, unconsciously, find stressful. Attempting tasks that may be difficult may just be too stressful. Perhaps it is easier and more satisfying to line up and put in order a few unruly toys.

He does like drying up the dishes but, on many occasions, I have found that he has returned them all to the washing-up bowl. Is this because he has forgotten to place them on the surface next to the sink? Perhaps he feels he would like to dry them up again? All the towels are carefully folded and the dishcloths, particularly the ones that are cut on the bias, are folded carefully. This last exercise is very challenging for most people but Peter has spent many hours perfecting the art and can now fold that type of cloth almost perfectly.

There are so many unanswered questions. But, I shall reflect on Danny's comment on his Granddad. Danny is eleven years old and has spent the last nine days here. He made this comment the day before he went home. It was unsolicited and therefore came completely out of the blue - or, more accurately, out of his head.

> "Grandma, I don't think there is really anything much the matter with Granddad. He can smile, he is polite and remembers his manners. He can eat nicely and looks kind. I like Granddad."

If a young boy can say this after a nine-day holiday here in this house, then I feel that I should take courage and regard Peter in the same way.

Perhaps if we are more accepting of what we have, and spend less time looking for things that are missing, then maybe the next few days, weeks, months or years will bring their own compensation.

I must still ask the question: 'Why, with all the anecdotal evidence which is available in homes like ours, do we not know more about the details, about the various stages, in dementia?' It is not enough to know the bald definition or headings of Stages one, two or three. We need to be aware of what is involved within each heading. Carers are in a position to provide some of this information to assist in intelligent research. Of course, the reason for the absence of information probably lies in that word 'funding.'

Thursday February 28th 2008

Apart from the vigorous and sustained sorting, lining up and folding of assorted items, there has been very little to distinguish today from the previous days of this month. It is definitely an appropriate time to redirect the focus of what we are trying to do. So the day looks as though a suitable ranking would be 8/10. It is just after midnight and Peter is asleep in bed. I can hardly believe my good fortune. It looks as though I shall soon have caught up with some sleep.

Chapter Four - Assessing skills, including our own

This would seem to be a good moment to consider some aspects of the point we have now reached, particularly as far as physical skills are concerned.

Dressing.

Provided the clothes are arranged, in order, on the chest of drawers Peter can, usually, manage to put his clothes on. Sometimes he needs help with his vest and socks. He struggles with the top button of his shirt and needs to be reminded to put on his tie. The tie takes a long time to fasten because it has to be lined up most carefully and the two ends have to meet at the same point. Things that he can't see will be more difficult to do. Lining up the tie is probably the bit of the tie he can see, so lining it up would be a sensible thing to do, rather like folding the tea towels. He can fasten his belt and button his jacket. He still tries to fasten his shoelaces and generally succeeds. He sometimes manages double bows - much to my dismay, as they are not easy to unfasten at one o'clock in the morning, while he is wriggling his foot.

Rachel has made the following observations, which are pertinent and helpful.

> "Clothing will only appear as serving different functions if you can recall why the appearance of one item is different from that of another. If you can no longer visualize what your arms look like - it will not be easy to recognize the clothing with sleeves. Lining up is necessary to help clarify when one item of clothing ends and another one begins.
>
> "The knowledge about when you are dressed, in pyjamas, or

even half dressed, is dependent on an intact proprioceptive system. This means that if Peter can no longer identify different sensations in his body, he will not feel that his legs are bare, cold etc., so, he will not be able to identify which bit of his body is dressed or not. If you do not hold a mental image of what you wear in the day, bare legs may not seem odd - especially if you are linking in with wearing school shorts or something similar."

Teeth

He can clean his own teeth, provided the toothpaste has been placed on the brush - and squashed flat to prevent it from falling off - and provided it is clearly visible on the washbasin. Very occasionally I have found him cleaning his teeth at other times of the day, but I do not yet know what triggers off that piece of behaviour. I measure out the mouthwash and stand with him for thirty seconds while he keeps it moving round his mouth. If he is distracted he simply swallows the mouthwash - without ill effect.

Shaving

Peter is very keen to shave and will do so whenever he sets eyes on the razor. It does have to be visible! He does finger his chin very frequently and is not happy if he detects even the slightest trace of stubble. I am not convinced that he would actually try and locate the razor, but he is definitely aware that he needs something to sort out the problem he has found with his face. If I produce the razor he greets it with enthusiasm and gets on with the shaving.

Hair

Peter does not actually comb his hair now - unless a comb is put into his hand - but he does check on it from time to time and indicates to me that he still has a good head of hair.

Undressing

This takes a great deal of time. The main problem is what to do with the clothes he has taken off. He knows how to put clothes on his body and he knows how to remove clothes from his body. What he does not know is what to do with the item in his hand. Consequently he tries to drape the item over any available surface. This can end up with items of clothing being carefully arranged on or over any of the bedroom furniture - excluding the bed. It is still strange to find these clothes so carefully folded and arranged, when he has spent most of the last seventy years oblivious to the fact that his clothes could be anywhere, other than screwed up in a disorderly heap and placed - or even dumped - in the nearest available space, be it bed, chest of drawers, chair or the wide expanse of carpeted floor. I wonder what would have happened if he had discovered this latent ability to fold clothes earlier in his life. It is an interesting thought, but does not solve the time-consuming problem of where he should put his clothes now. If I take him into the bathroom, show him the laundry basket on the chair, and then ask him to undress and put his clothes in the basket, he does try to respond. This will only work if I show him his pyjamas hanging on the door of the airing cupboard. He knows that he has to put those on after his bath, even though putting them on is more than a little challenging.

Rachel's observation:

> "These skills are going to go soon too. Dad is currently accessing some patterned-in responses, such as reaching for the handle on the door in order to get his pyjamas. This would suggest that there is still a link with a bath and new clothes. He probably wouldn't respond any differently if

you were to hang different clothing on the door handle now. A few months ago he would have reacted differently because they would have 'felt wrong,' but that does not apply at the stage we have now reached."

Bathing

I am still having to point to the water in the bath and say that he needs to get into the water, sit down and wash himself. He does try and wash himself, but only the parts he can see. He has stopped trying to reach his back or his neck. Neither does he do much with his feet. So it is very important to have plenty of deep-cleansing foam in the bath - to reach those parts he cannot see. At the moment I am leaving him to wash himself, because his autism means he does not like being touched. He does like to stretch out in the bath, so the water does touch all of him. Given half a chance he would try and put soap on his hair and then splash bath water over it. This is not allowed! So, when I wash his hair - which he does not like - I take the opportunity to wash his back as well. His skin seems to be very clean and healthy.

Toenails

These are so very hard to control. Peter makes a great deal of fuss because it is impossible to cut toenails without touching the skin. Also the toenails are very hard to cut. Currently I am trying to soften them with a proprietary nail-softener, but I am not too optimistic about any improvement in the situation. Scissors seem to be quicker and easier to use than clippers - but only on softish nails.

Eating and Drinking

Peter enjoys his food and eats whatever I put in front of him. He has difficulty in cutting up his food, so I now serve him food like pasta spirals, peas, beans, soft potato, tomato and sweet corn. He has chicken breast - cooked in a casserole - or quorn in its several forms. This is served in a cheese, mushroom, or tomato-based sauce which has helped to overcome a slight initial problem with swallowing. The food is easy to eat - using a spoon - nutritious, and is enjoyed. What more is required? He is much more interested in drinking my coffee than in drinking his own. This is somewhat odd as the two are identical. However he rarely finishes a drink so it is very important to keep an eye on how many half-full cups are about at any given time. He eats and drinks when food and drink are on offer, but very rarely indicates that he would like something to eat or drink.

Rachel has made the following observations.

> "He still recognises the function of cutlery.
> He recognises edible versus inedible.
> He is able to locate food on the plate.
> He can navigate round the plate to collect up food.
> He is able to close his lips round the utensil and create a good lip seal.
> He still has the grinding action of molars, but biting and tearing are reduced.
> He does not have a mature chew.
> The swallow reflex is triggered, although it appears weaker. There is some evidence of residue in the pharynx post swallow. This may be heard in a slightly wet voice after drinking and eating. This clears within a minute.
> He remains sitting while eating.
> His response to tastes does not seem hugely altered, though does he perhaps have a sweeter tooth now?
> He still enjoys food when presented with it.
> Once he has started he will eat the meal without any prompts.
> Having said that, it is still necessary, at times, to remind him

that the food on the plate is for *him* to eat and he does not have to share it with Katy or anyone else.

Drinks are less likely to be finished - I am not sure why with drinks and not with food, unless, once the cup has been put down it is out of sight and mind. The cutlery remains in the hands and so serves as a reminder of the job in hand?"

Toileting

Peter is still independent and generally remembers to wash his hands after using the toilet. What a silly expression! He does not often remember the essential word 'flush' - but that is because he seems to be very confused as to what he is supposed to do to with the cistern. Sometimes he takes the lid off and inspects the ball cock. Sometimes he comes to 'tell' me that there is a problem I need to solve. He seems very surprised by the sudden rush of water resulting from depressing the handle - but he does not remember how to repeat the trick. Perhaps we should both try harder.

Mobility

He can walk round the house and climb up the stairs - using the extra handrail. Peter walks with a characteristic - for him - lurch. I have noticed, over the last few weeks, that he is walking in a very lop-sided manner, is very tottery a lot of the time and has to steady himself when getting up from his chair. Once he has started walking around the house he seems to become a little steadier. Peter can wash and dry the dishes and then line them up on any surface in the kitchen. He spends a significant amount of time in organising and reorganising certain sections of his library of books. The ones he generally reorganises are Pevsner's *Buildings of Britain*, his maps, his books on Archbishop Thomas Cranmer and those on Church Architecture.

Speech and Conversation

He has very little intelligible conversation. It tends to be restricted to "You, me, where" which means, "Is there anyone else in the house?" Perhaps I should qualify that and say that very little is intelligible to us. He does say, quite clearly, words such as "Hello," "Ah," "Yes" and "No," "I do not like," and "Oh, Thank you." He can spend a considerable amount of time making sounds which I feel I should be able to understand. It sounds quite normal and is accompanied by hand gestures - which usually look as though he is indicating measurements and/or directions. It is simply beyond my comprehension. Depending on the general intonation of his talking I respond with appropriate sounds of approval, agreement and/or encouragement, until I sense that he has finished whatever he has been trying to say. Sometimes he knows that he has not made himself clear and appears to be disappointed. On other occasions he is well pleased with his achievement. I am going to ask Rachel to make some professional observations at this stage so we know exactly what we are supposed to be doing - or seeing - or understanding.

Rachel's Observations:

> "We can divide Dad's communication in a number of ways. It probably isn't helpful to think about verbal and non-verbal communication, but rather to think of the different functions his communication is serving.
>
> "**Facial expressions**. These he uses for greeting people, accepting and refusing offers of food and drink.
>
> "**Gestures**. These are readily used for responding to most situations and also indicating when he has not understood what has been said. He shrugs his shoulders and looks somewhat pained.

"**Vocalisations**. There are many, many vocalisations - most of which are now incomprehensible. This is the favoured way of commenting on whatever he thinks he would like to discuss.

"**Jargon or Nonsense**. Sadly there is far too much of this but it is generally worth persevering, in case something emerges - it is also an element of polite behaviour! This might preserve the dignity of the Carer as well as the Cared For.

"**Words and phrases**. Social phrases, such as *Please* and *Thank you* are still appropriately used, as are greetings, *Yes* and *No, Who* and *What.*"

There have been so many changes in the amount of language Peter understands; now we need to keep track of the words and actions. It is useful to us for Peter still to be able to understand in order for him to help us.

He is still capable of linking names to objects, such as items of clothing, scissors, comb and toothbrush. He also knows the function of these named items - which is most helpful!

He also responds, with understanding, to verbs and phrases such as 'Put down,' 'Stand up,' 'Well done' and 'Stop.'

To maximise Peter's use of language, it is most helpful to try and maintain, wherever appropriate, a smiling face and a pleasant tone of voice. We also need to keep track of his understanding of the function of key objects as, for example, when he no longer understands the function of a spoon, that would be the time when he is going to need to be fed.

The Brain

This is really the area I am most interested in monitoring, so I am going to consider the current level of Peter's skills within his daily activities of relaxation and pleasure.

Reading

What is going on in his head when he sits in the chair for one or even two hours in the evening? There is very little evidence of the turning of a page, so I do not know whether he is enjoying sitting in the chair with a book in his hand, or whether he is enjoying looking at the print and the pictures. It may be that he is slowly decoding in a way that he finds satisfying. Perhaps it would be fair to say that Peter is still capable of decoding not only simple words but also some relatively complex words. There is little sign of reading with comprehension. But he has spent his whole life surrounded by the books he has collected, so perhaps he now finds looking at those books both soothing and comforting. I have no means of knowing, but I would like to think he is choosing to do this himself. The books tend to be held the right way up and are treated respectfully and carefully. Again it would be true to say that, during the course of an afternoon, he appears to be making sufficient progress in order to be able to be satisfied with what he is doing. I wonder if any of the words make any real sense to him. Sometimes he looks at an architectural photograph and then points and holds his hands as if he were demonstrating some important detail. On the other hand his world has shrunk so much that perhaps there is little room for knowledge.

What does go on in the mind?

How much is restricted to the satisfaction of physical needs in order to survive?

Where does imagination and spirituality find an expression?

At one stage there was a very real fear concerning almost everything that was going on around him. Now that fear and anxiety has disappeared - which is a great relief. I can only say that a passive calm has taken over and left a seemingly blank space somewhere else in Peter's tiny little world.

Writing

Peter has almost lost this skill. This is mainly due to the simple fact of not having to do any writing. He cannot sign his name independently but he can copy the letters if written clearly and separately. This is a very slow and laborious process because he keeps losing the letter when he turns from the written word to the paper on which he is trying to write. There is no interest in the activity and, now we no longer sign cheques, the times when a signature would be required are very few indeed. He was not able to sign his name in 2007 in order to qualify for a postal vote. As he has no knowledge of what voting is all about, there seemed to be no real reason for claiming a postal vote for Peter in order that I could have two votes.

Arithmetic - of course one must include Arithmetic!

Peter has not been able to handle money for the last two years but, until six months ago, he could line up £1 coins and 50p pieces and so 'help' Tom to count the church collection. When he was last able to go to church he was not able to sort the coins into groups of £10 - because he could not manage the counting sequence.

Relationships.

Peter cannot identify the members of his family but he does sort them by size. So we have 'Big ones' - hand held high above his head - and

'Small ones' - hand held down to his knees. I am recognised as the one who looks after him, but he is not always sure about where I live. Sometimes he tries to ask when I will be leaving. I tend to avoid giving a definite answer! Rachel is also recognised as someone who has a rightful place in the care system. She may not be too pleased about that! But old habits die hard and so Peter will welcome anyone who comes to the house and is always keen to shake hands - especially with the window-cleaner and the plumber. He also likes to measure his height against the height of visitors - especially tall visitors. I am realising how difficult it is to quantify intellectual skills when they have been brutally attacked by dementia.

Making sense of what he sees

Peter spends a lot of time examining objects, views from the window and rearranging - or even re-ordering - his possessions. He cannot seem to make much sense of the television. This is a problem for Peter rather than for the Television Companies. Because he does not hear very well, he cannot match what is being said to what is happening on the screen. This results in frustration and he does not wish the television to be intruding into his space. We can all sympathise with that! Very occasionally I can find a programme or a DVD - generally about architecture and/or churches and cathedrals - about which he has some knowledge or recall and so will not need any sound to support it. If Peter's brain is able to drag out some relevant information then he can enjoy whatever is on offer without the conflict of sound.

Making sense of what he hears

I sometimes feel that there is an elective or even a selective element in his hearing problem. I keep wondering why he appears to be able to hear me when I am talking quietly on the phone, or talking with friends, and yet he cannot hear the television or classical music - unless the volume is turned up. This does not work for long because he seems to be very sensitive to the slightest variation in dynamics and, straightaway, the louder parts will be intrusive and he will want the sound removed.

Peter seldom understands the very simple instructions I give and he certainly cannot understand any very simple request I might make. Consequently conversations tend to be one-sided or even non-existent.

Rachel's response:

> "The inconsistency in responses to the auditory environment may well be a result of not knowing what to tune into and what to ignore. Responding to the phone will have had other cues to go with it, e.g. the sound of movement towards the phone, repetition of the ringing tone."

This is probably enough to start off with. The ranking for the day will continue as before, using the old criteria, which is designed to give an over-all picture. The second part will be to note carefully any change from the broad outline contained on these pages. Any such changes should be noted in the daily diary and perhaps we will see some picture emerging over the next few months.

Chapter Five - Which is dominated by questions

Thursday March 6th 2008

Today has been an excellent day by any standards. Peter was ready to get up soon after 2.00 pm and, again, was able to put on his own pants, trousers and socks. He has changed his reading book. Now he is enjoying *Britain from the Air* and is studying it quite intently. I am still no wiser as to how much he is taking into his brain but I hope there is something! The day can be ranked as 9/10. I feel that we are on an easy path at the moment and I hope and pray that nothing happens to alter what is a worthwhile way of living - for both of us. Peter seems happy and contented and I am able to fit in all the domestic demands and, because of Peter's waking hours, or rather his sleeping hours, I can still go and visit the people who need to be visited and collect up those who need to be collected up. I feel that I am a very normal person living a very normal life.

Friday March 14th 2008

There was an interesting meeting with Debi this morning. We talked about some of the issues raised by changing the focus of what we thought we were trying to achieve in the daily recording, and came to the conclusion that there is very little real information on the whole subject of Alzheimer's disease. We are able to understand what might be happening in the brain cells, but there seems very little information on why some things happen. I am still left feeling that there is a great deal of detailed and interesting information which could be accessed, if only carers had somewhere to place records of what they experience, on a daily basis, when caring for their charges. Using the facilities of the Internet offered me nothing useful. Am I naive in thinking that there are three stages we could be considering, before the explosion of this disease in the not too distant future? It is surely inevitable, as the population of older people increases and cerebral atrophy affects more and more people. The three stages I would like to explore are as follows:

1 What is happening?

The evidence is before our very eyes - an apt enough quote in this situation.

2 Why is it happening? What is the brain doing?

This could be considered by the medical experts.

3 How do we manage the behaviour?

This can only be achieved when carers and - at some of the stages - people with the disease, can be helped to make sense of what is going on.

To return to the subject of this record. The day has been very good with Peter showing his brilliance in lining up and folding up tea-towels. He has enjoyed the day and been very calm. I will note, for the record, that at 5.35 this morning he was wandering round the house. He was being extremely quiet and, when I tracked him down in the Study, he seemed to be creeping around - almost on tip-toe! I went into the Study but he was completely unaware of my presence so I went quietly back to bed. He returned to bed a few minutes later - again in an uncharacteristically quiet manner - and went to sleep. I think the day deserves 8/10 - it is better to rank the day before the bath/bed pantomime starts.

Wednesday March 19th 2008

I awoke at 7.00 am to find a very cold space next to me. On searching the house I found Peter sleeping in one of the children's beds. Either I am sleeping more deeply or Peter is now creeping quietly around and not bumping into things. Either is somewhat inconvenient! On my return from the early morning school run I found Peter back in our bed and sleeping soundly - which he did until 11.45 am. He has spent ninety minutes trying to make a small mirror fit into its outer frame. It refused to fit so Peter has placed each item in a different part of the kitchen. Does this mean something? Perhaps the two items do not match. Perhaps on the other hand, the two items have to be separated instead of being joined together. Who knows?

Rachel came to sit with Peter tonight while I went to the Police Choir Practice. She reported an uneventful evening - apart from the theft, by Peter, of her tea. Her tea consisted of a pot of yogurt. Peter ate it because it was visible in the kitchen and was pleased to present her with the thoroughly licked lid. In view of Rachel's enforced generosity I feel compelled to award the day a resounding 9/10. Nothing that happens now can be more disconcerting than the unexpected loss of one's tea.

Tuesday March 25th 2008

There has been a most interesting programme on the TV tonight. It was *Horizon*'s presentation of memory and how it works. Naturally Alzheimer's disease was included in the programme, as was one remarkable, sensible lady, whose husband was diagnosed with the disease seven years ago, when he was 58 years old. Amongst some other basic and sensible observations she focused our attention on the following comment: 'When someone has Alzheimer's disease it is as though he or she is dying from the inside out.'

I thought it a most apt comment, because it sums up exactly what is happening to someone who may look well from the outside, and yet is in the process of losing every single part of his or her personality and being.

Thursday April 3rd 2008

2.10 pm - and with great reluctance - Peter rose from his bed.

Last night's little performance really takes some beating, although I have to say that some of it was my own silly fault. At 12.15 am, I decided to set the ball rolling for bedtime - even though Peter was most reluctant to understand anything I was saying. Twice he put his clothes back on his body after I had helped him take them off. The first time he was standing next to the bath, wearing his socks, shoes, vest and pants under his pyjamas. Having removed them again he climbed into the bath and sprinkled some water over his knees. So far, so good. He was soon dried and dressed in his pyjamas. I thought he was ready to get into bed so I left him for a few minutes to open and close some drawers - which thing he likes to do - and then I returned. He was wearing his shoes and socks, his shirt and tie and his jersey. All on top of his pyjamas. We started the striptease again and put the clothes in a safe place - but not safe enough! Stupidly, I left him in bed while I went to have a bath. I could hear a lot of moving about and so was aware that he might have been doing some re-ordering of the drawers. How wrong could I be? Very, very wrong! When I went into the bedroom Peter was dressed in his shoes and socks, his vest and pants - under his pyjamas - his shirt and tie - under his pyjama top - with his warm jersey on top. I abandoned the struggle to remove the day clothing and moved into the children's room and got into bed. He was wandering around, switching the lights on and off, opening and closing doors and generally being less than quiet. So I placed the beanbag against the door and got back into bed. It was 2.25am. He wandered along to the bathroom and tried to push my door open. Needless to say, the beanbag was more determined than Peter so I was able to close my eyes and go to sleep. I awoke, totally refreshed, at 6.30am.

When I went in to see if Peter was still in bed, soon after 7.30am, I found him neatly arranged in bed, wearing the clothes I have already described, clutching the duvet and covered with the heavy brown velvet bedspread. He had retrieved the bedspread from the floor and placed it carefully back on the bed. I checked to see if he was still wearing his shoes. He was not. I felt a deep admiration for the self-restraint of the human brain in some difficult situations. We have also had a lovely day with Joe and Amber. The holiday will soon come to an unwelcome end! But Peter has been extraordinarily calm today. The day looks as though it could qualify for a 9/10, so I do hope the clothing situation is less fraught tonight. It is very evident that the sight of any article of clothing creates a problem for Peter. I must remember to remove the laundry basket from the bathroom the minute Peter gets into the bath. Then, with luck, he will only be interested in the clothes he can see before his very eyes - i.e. his pyjamas.

Friday April 11th 2008

Rising time was 2.00 pm.

It sounds a little like reporting on the time of the high tide!

Today I decided that, as I was needing to go out to Assembly at St. Mary's School at 2.30 pm, I would see what would happen if I left Peter to get on independently. I only had to help him with his vest and he then seemed to be moving on the right path. Astonishingly - or perhaps one should not be astonished - he came down just before 2.30 pm with his clothes on and his tie round his neck. I was most impressed and wondered if the ease of the previous day had any bearing on his responses today. Or perhaps I was not making so many mistakes in my management of the situation. I left him with his breakfast and found, on my return with the children, that he had eaten his breakfast and washed up his cereal bowl, spoon and cup. The only thing he had ignored was the toothbrush - complete with a measure of toothpaste. He has been busy this evening looking at his book on *Renaissance Architecture* and trying to measure the height of the Fugger Chapel, in Germany. He is doing his best to make sounds the rest of us can understand. Perhaps if I were to sit here long enough I would make sense of what he is saying, but, for all sorts of worthy and unworthy reasons, I cannot quite do that. I have realised that, in most situations, if Peter is going to achieve anything independently, he is most likely to succeed if he does everything in his own time and without pressure - offered as encouragement - from me. The only reason we cannot achieve more is that each action takes an inordinately long time. Consequently we all run out of time and Peter runs out of steam. If we can continue in this fashion, today will rank as a second 10/10 - and, who knows, this may just become the norm! After all, the most astonishing things can happen. The day has ended remarkably well and I am reckoning on being in bed soon after 12.30 am - after a ride on the bike. Unlike our trip in 1995, when using plane and coach, it now takes a very short time to reach Jerusalem - when travelling, as I am now, by bicycle. I will just call in on one of those Arab villages.

Bethany is a good place to choose. As with most Arab villages it is not a place of great wealth, but, what it lacks in wealth, it more than makes up for in places of interest. The ruins of the Byzantine and Crusader churches are very much in evidence - as is a series of underground caves. Our first descent would be to visit the cave which is generally regarded as being the Tomb of Lazarus - cousin of Jesus. The day was exceedingly hot and the sun exceedingly bright. At last it was time to take our turn in the queue. It was, I hasten to say, a very small queue. The first stage was to try and negotiate a very narrow and uneven flight of stone steps which, we were promised, would take us down to a small rock chamber. Standing at the top of the steps was a very pleasant Arab lady holding a tray of small candles. Having equipped ourselves with a lighted candle - on a take it now and pay later basis - we prepared to follow the four people in front of us. I was amazed to find everything so dark. It was quite impossible to see anything at all, except the vague flickering of the candle. How on earth was anyone supposed to find any of the steps. I was in the middle of the procession and the going was exceedingly slow. Not only was it slow but I felt that I was trying to walk in mid-air. I could not begin to think how Peter was managing, as balance and co-ordination could sometimes cause him a problem. The whole situation felt completely out of my control and more than a little threatening. It was at that precise moment that my brain started to clear and the grey cells started working again. The way forward was now clear. One action was called for and I acted with all speed. Quietly and unobtrusively, taking care not to draw anyone's attention to what was about to happen, I took off my sunglasses and found that the way forward was indeed clear. The descent was accomplished with alacrity - which must have been a great relief to the people behind me. After looking, with great interest, at the cave of the Tomb of Lazarus, we retraced our steps - and the stone ones - and emerged, blinking and puffing, into the sunlight. The candles were paid for, sunglasses reattached to noses and we returned to travel along the Jericho road. Before returning to Denton I am going to recall the sight of a shepherdess, wearing her traditional dress, and, following the Palestinian custom, leading her sheep from the front. In this country shepherds tend to drive the sheep from the back - while a sheepdog might be used to lead from the front.

Denton calls again so I shall rejoin the desert road and head for home.

Tuesday April 15th 2008

And never assume that which should never be assumed - particularly when a visit to the dentist has been included on the agenda for the day!

There had been very little enthusiasm for co-operating this morning and Peter was certainly not in any mood to move - other than at an extremely elderly snail's extremely slow pace. Having arrived at the surgery and having been ushered into the treatment room, the chair had then to be negotiated. Firstly, Peter did not want to be parted from his great-coat. This meant that sitting down in the dentist's chair would be slightly more difficult, as the fairly rigid suede-effect coat would occupy a good amount of space. Space is one of the things Peter finds very difficult. I was trying to see how he planned to bypass the dental equipment and other fixtures and fittings which, to be fair, would have presented a significant challenge to those of us trying to negotiate without Alzheimer's or Autism. For Peter it was very challenging. He did not, of course, find himself able to respond to an arm on his arm. But, when he eventually sat down and the dentist was able to contemplate the job ahead, I witnessed something bordering on the astonishing. Having settled himself into the chair Peter then opened his mouth - without being asked - and allowed the dental inspection to take place. The mild-mannered dentist said, "Close. Rinse." Peter did those two things and then opened his mouth again - without being asked. Once the inspection was over, and the quality of the brushing had been praised, Peter then climbed out of the chair, with no sign of difficulty, and shook the dentist warmly by both hands! No further treatment was required this time so we paid the £15 fee and left the surgery. My immediate thought was "How on earth had Peter been able to co-operate at this level, without the need for any word or other assistance?" Bearing in mind how difficult it is to achieve much in the way of sensible co-operation, what I witnessed - and the dentist found worthy of comment - seemed little short of amazing. So how did it happen? I hope someone can provide me with a reasoned answer. The day has to be a 9/10 day because of the high level of unconscious co-operation at the dental surgery. It is now midnight but, as there is no sign of the day ending, I shall ride my bicycle.

Wednesday April 30th 2008

Rising time 1.50 pm.

A day worthy of a 10/10 ranking. We shall also celebrate an actual conclusion for this stage in the writing. I feel very pleased with its completion and feel we have all learnt something.

So what *has* been learned so far? The quick answer has to be - a great deal.

1. The first and most important point is that one should equip oneself with one or more of the following items before embarking on a similar enterprise.

a) A punch bag.
b) A rowing machine.
c) An exercise bike has been known, in this household, to have oiled stormy waters.

2. On reading the text again I am conscious of the fact that it may have the makings of a fairly successful pantomime script. Perhaps, as this is a recording of a real life experience, it does reflect, more or less faithfully, the reality that life is somewhat similar to the pantomime element contained within the more successful forms of farce.

3. It has also been pointed out, on more than one occasion, that it may be counterproductive to try and investigate the minutiae of the behaviour of dementia, but I would disagree with that idea on several levels. First, it may be very helpful to spend time looking for any patterns of behaviour which may then, in turn, be examined to see if there is common factor in the causes and/or effects of the behaviour. Perhaps I should elaborate on this particular point. Over the six-month period I have seen a definite move from depression and

anxiety to a calmer and less stressed way of being. Peter has, possibly, moved further down the Alzheimer slope, but I am now in a position to be able to recognise the subtleties of further changes because, with Peter, there is a similar pattern of loss of concentration each time his condition deteriorates. I feel that I know, rather more accurately, exactly what I am dealing with and am more able to take appropriate action and use appropriate strategies when the need arises. The complexities of Autism, coupled with those of Alzheimer's disease, have to be managed most carefully when it comes to dressing, hair-washing and accepting the high level of repetitive behaviour. I thought I had worked out the demands of Autism, but I was not fully equipped when it came to dealing with Alzheimer's as well. Either one would have been enough. To have both rather smacks of greed or exaggeration. But looking carefully at what has been going on for twenty-four hours a day, seven days a week for the last six months of a period spanning no less than eight years, has provided me with much food for thought.

4. The style of writing had to be considered most carefully, so that the end result, namely the reading of the account, would be achieved in a helpful, informative and appropriate manner. This has meant looking at what was being recorded in a positive way. It would be very easy to succumb to the frustration of hours of tedium, seemingly silly behaviour, no conversation and limited communication. But, I have discovered that, contained within each and every day - even 1/10 or cancelled days - has been some tiny nugget of gold. There has always been something about which one could laugh, or at least smile. This recognition that there is something good about every day does much to preserve the dignity and character of the person being cared for. It also does much to preserve the sanity and balance of mind of the person doing the caring. I would like to think that the positive aspect of the day is an achievement on the part of the person being cared for. It may work on both sides. It may be that achievement is because

of the way the carer has managed the day or a challenging situation. In which case the carer has achieved as well. Without the carer that particular achievement might never have been possible. So perhaps a modest pat on the back would be in order and a very big pat on the back for all the support, both practical and prayerful, from people who work so hard to keep us afloat. You will know if I mean you, because you will be reading this page. Thank you.

5. I have noticed, as a result of what I am going to call this *study*, that, almost without exception, the major difficulties have arisen because of mismanagement or insensitive handling on my part. This is not a case of self-flagellation, but it is a case of being able to stand back from the situation and see what, if anything, could have been done to change the outcome. On a practical level I have learnt not to kneel down in front of Peter when unfastening his shoes because, in that position, I appear to be a threat and he kicks out with his feet. If I position myself to one side I can take however long it takes to untie double bows - and sometimes that can be a long time! Another very important point, when helping Peter to take off his pyjama jacket and put on his vest, is to make sure that there are no sudden or jerky movements when touching the clothes or the skin, as this can initiate a lashing-out reaction. This is the problem of Autism rather than Alzheimer's but it has to be managed properly.

6. Another point has become very apparent, which may not be very obvious to people not closely connected with the problem. It is very difficult to understand or accept that people with Alzheimer's do not learn new habits or simple skills for survival. Having written that, I can see the obvious error. We all know, and accept, that people are unique individuals, and what works for one person may not work with another. If you know your own individual really well, and have studied his or her changing moods, you will be able to adapt to the deteriorating condition with less emotional damage to yourself - and

consequently to the person for whom you are caring.

7. I have at last learnt and accepted that there is no way in which Peter can be hurried. Now that he has no apparent understanding of the passage of time he is not able to work out the concept of slow or fast/quick as far as his day is concerned. This will inevitably extend to the daily routine and any activities which may be attempted. Any pressure only causes upset and the potential for aggression - neither of which is necessary in this equation.

8. I only put out the clothing, in the correct order, that Peter is going to wear each day. Any extra clothes will be put on the body, irrespective of suitability or even the normal order for wearing such clothing. Pyjama tops on top of a dark jacket may seem to be a good idea but, as far as sartorial elegance is concerned, it has very little to commend it.

9. The same applies to food. Any food left lying about will be consumed because Peter has no idea as to whether or not he has eaten anything within the last minute or two. As he is losing weight a few extra calories may be a good thing but it is not helpful to find half-eaten items tucked away in odd places. So be generous at all times, but do know exactly where you have put tomorrow's dinner.

10. Watches, wallets, fragile ornaments and other treasured possessions are also best kept under close supervision - lest they be whisked away, and lined up somewhere inaccessible to you.

11. I have also learnt how essential it is to keep wearing a smile, because this sometimes triggers off an attempt at conversation. It may not be comprehensible but sometimes there is a surprise: e.g. the day he suddenly announced, "I am a priest. Where is my Church?" He did not wait for an answer but the question was clear enough. Something had popped up in his brain. I cannot rule out a

possible connection, at any time, between his brain and his environment - so I shall continue to listen out for something sensible! Any half constructed comments serve as a reminder that the real person is still there, even though he is concealed, to some extent, by Alzheimer's. It may well be that he does not relish the situation any more than we do.

12. So, as we flit in and out of Peter's particular land of shadows, we would do well to remember that it is not - as yet - our own environment   Hold on to your own world, take most things with a pinch of salt and always use a most generous quantity of common sense. Therein lies hope in Keeping Going.

Rachel's Contribution:

> "You made a conscious decision to make the most of the times when you can leave the house and attend to your other five jobs of work. In order to achieve a level of productivity and normality you have engineered the day so that Dad takes as long as he takes to get into bed, and, in return, you let him sleep for as long as you require him to for you to achieve what has been demanded of you during the day. Had you not done this you would have been forced to have carer support, and there might well have been more incidents of aggression.

> "You have stuck to your minimum standards, for example over baths and independent teeth cleaning. Others may have suggested that a bath a day is not the be all and end all, but it maintains what is normal in this family, and one by which you judge the standard of care you are providing.

> "The daily recording of happenings has also allowed both of us to take a step back and view Dad's 'case' from time to

time. This has enabled both of us to apply a little grey matter to a situation that otherwise only triggers those more negative emotions, such as rage, fear, sadness and loss.

"The more subtle changes we need to be looking at will become more physical in nature over time. The daily reports have captured the subtlety of communicative and behavioural shifts and drops. What we are beginning to see now are changes in mobility, motor function, physical sensations and the ability to respond to these. In addition there will be subtle increases in jerks and other neurological features that will be easily missed if we are not on the alert. Pain and discomfort may be harder to spot, and will require the knowledge used with babies at a pre-intentional level. Many of these changes are missed in other people, but, once you have established your own vocabulary for what you are seeing, these too will serve as important indicators, as and when changes in Dad's 'care plan' are called for."

Stage Two

Chapter One - In which we discover the importance of folding and sorting

Thursday May 1st 2008

As already planned, it has been decided to expand the scope of the writing, in order to include some more specific areas of the way Alzheimer's disease is affecting Peter's ability to have some sort of control over his life. Although there seems little reason to suppose that there is much personal control over what he is able to do with his life, it is incumbent on the people responsible for his care and well-being to ensure that the quality of his life is compromised as little as possible by the disease. This is not easy and there seems little reason to expect to find many answers to our many questions. However, it is only by trying to find some sort of understanding of what is happening, that we shall be able to cope with whatever lies in store. Fortunately we are not able to see what this will amount to, so we can take each day as it comes and make of it what we can. In this way we can hold onto our own ability to cope - sometimes known as sanity!

One of the benefits of the last six months has been the opportunity to spend time recording and perhaps understanding the changes in Peter's behaviour. I certainly feel that I am in a position to notice, fairly quickly, any significant change in what he does - and how he does it. So, the ranking will continue but there will be no accompanying commentary, as I shall be working on the original criteria - such as it is. Rachel and I will be looking at language and mobility - just in case it helps in doing the job more efficiently and with a little more understanding. Even if we cannot work more effectively we might learn a little more. I have now realised that there is very little hope of spreading this particular message 'on a wider screen' but that should not invalidate the object of the exercise - which is to Keep Going. There is also every possibility that this stage will be much less wordy than Stage One - unless I become quite carried away of course.

Friday May 2nd 2008

The day itself has a ranking of 8/10 - according to the old criteria.

I propose looking at the two chosen areas - mobility and language - very carefully - and so will need to consider the most appropriate way to view and record the current state, along with subsequent variations.

Monday May 5th 2008

I am tempted to try a new experiment, in which I leave Peter to get up at his preferred time - if such a time exists - and dress in his own time. This time will be recorded as the *Rising time* and might just be very helpful in the long term. In a way, time for Peter has ceased to have any relevance. Perhaps, provided I can run a timetable for my own particular commitments, this house can dance to the *tune* and, most especially, to the *time* of Peter's particular needs - rather along the lines of demand feeding for the very young. I am interested in trying to follow this line because I do feel that I am becoming a little less patient, whenever I am trying to fit Peter into a timetable - which I will have set to suit *my* needs. Perhaps Peter's needs have nothing to do with conventional timekeeping. On second thoughts, I shall continue to set the latest acceptable time for starting the bath/bed nightmare. All the time it exists as a nightmare I shall have to make it fit in with what I can actually manage - as far as patience is concerned. There should be a merry quip upon which to end this paragraph but, for the moment, it eludes me. So, let us end with the ranking - which is an astounding 9/10. Being able to work in the garden for two successive days has not only transformed the garden but it has also transformed the internal machinations of the house - including the ranking. Perhaps this is telling us something we need to know and will such knowledge allow us to continue with the transformation?

Saturday May 10th 2008

Rising time 2.05 pm.

A difficult day - no really obvious reason, except that Peter's comprehension of what is going on around him has been at an all time low, so a mere 1/10 is probably justified.

Monday May 12th 2008

Rising time 2.05pm.

Today has been an outstandingly good day. Peter has asked me, "Are you there?" and "Are you well?" Both observations were very clear and were accompanied by a smiling face! I am tempted to say the day deserves at least 10/10. So we have some language. Tomorrow I shall search for some mobility.

Thursday May 15th 2008

Rising time 1.50 pm.

I must mention that, after a very successful and reasonably managed bath and bed-time, Peter went to sleep for one hour, before waking up and testing out his mobility. He spent no less than one hour walking round, through, past and into all the upstairs rooms. Of course there are only five upstairs rooms but, with an astonishing display of skill, he managed to create the illusion of inspecting and checking out at least twelve rooms. The idea, as far as I could fathom out, was to switch on as many lights for as many times as was possible. After that he had to try to sort out the contents of the chest of drawers and - this is a new departure - the contents of both wardrobes. All this investigation took place in the dark as I had removed the light bulb days ago. Then, at just after three o'clock he finished walking and inspecting and got into bed. One of the points one is forced to accept is that it is totally impossible to ask Peter to stop, or even finish, walking around and moving things from here to there. He just does not understand. Neither does he have any idea of what he is doing. Consequently there is no possible alternative to waiting, as quietly and patiently as possible, until he has stopped. It is a most challenging situation and one hopes for a long interval before it happens again. There is absolutely no reasoning with Peter over anything at all. We have had plenty of mobility but where has that left the language? A little after seven o'clock this evening Peter stood at the kitchen door and looked out at the garden. "Very fine!" he said. We admired the garden and then moved into the Study. He then stood in front of the big tapestry and said again "Very fine!" So there we had two appropriate comments, which gave us both pleasure. It has been very quiet since then. If I thought we were going to have an undisturbed and quiet night I would give the day 10/10.

Friday May 16th 2008

Rising time - an incredible 4.15 pm.

Yesterday moved quickly into today as bed-time proved to be slow and tedious but, at least, the sleeping hours were spent in sleeping and not in wandering around!

Peter has been very good indeed since his late arising. He came into the garden while I was cutting the grass and spent a happy few minutes gathering leaves from the lawn. He also said, in a very clear voice, "What shall I do?" I wonder if I am hearing more phrases now that they are the focus of my attention. That would make some sort of sense. He is very, very slow in moving around the house and in any physical activity he undertakes. That does not seem to have been changed by being under scrutiny. It is harder for him to take off his clothes, mainly because he is generally weaker and each manoeuvre requires more effort. He is still doing up his shirt buttons, fastening his belt and fastening his shoe laces. A single bow for the right shoe and a double bow for the left. I wonder why? The day deserves 9/10.

Saturday May 17th 2008

Rising time 2.15 pm.

Peter has been in a happy frame of mind and, although I have not heard too much in the way of language, he has done a lot of walking around. We are enjoying a period of peace and contentment. This in itself should be a focus for scrutiny. Perhaps we could catch hold of this stage, understand why it is happening and then create and re-create the conditions which cause it to happen. Although I fear this might be wishful thinking. Perhaps we should enjoy the time while it is here. That is exactly what we shall do and award today a ranking of 10/10.

Monday May 19th 2008

Rising time 1.35 pm.

In order to pull this stage of the account into some sort of shape I intend listing the words I hear and check on the context. Then I shall ask Rachel to analyse the list and interpret anything that can be interpreted.

Yes. No. Thank you.
Please. (This seems to be used when asking for something not to happen.)
Very good. You. Me.
I don't know. What shall I do?
Where is? How?

These words seem to me to be the basic words needed for survival in any environment. But I shall leave the last word to the expert.

You are the expert, Rachel, so prepare to enlighten us, please.

> **"Yes, No, Very Good.** These are words that I would categorize as automatic speech - stored in a different place within the brain from planned speech.
>
> **"Please,** when used in the context of saying 'No' may be automatic, but seems to be said with more understanding about what he is saying no (or please) to. It may be a response that comes when he is feeling threatened or scared in some way. I certainly believe that there are times, when I have been attempting to encourage him to comply with my requests, when he has looked at me with fear and his response has been one of desperation.
>
> **"You** and **Me** are encouraging - they suggest an awareness of self and others; they are of course very early words to develop along with Yes and No.
>
> **"I don't know** and **What shall I do** suggest planned language in some way and may appear at moments of increased awareness.
>
> **"Where is it** and **How:** these are odd because,

developmentally, **How** is a really difficult concept and one of the last question words to develop.

"**How** could be used to mean "I have no idea what you are asking me to do."

"As you say, they are all words that are key to Peter surviving in his world."

Wednesday May 21st 2008

Rising time 2.15 pm

Peter has spent much of the day wandering around but, on balance, I think he might have regarded it as a rather productive sort of day. It might even be regarded as pleasurable. He has arranged many tea towels in orderly piles and has measured out several glasses and cups of water. He has lined up pencils and picked up a pocketful of leaves from the lawn. This is a relatively new activity. He used to enjoy picking up the rubbish in the Park but he was also interested in putting his collection in a bin. These days he likes to store them in his jacket pocket - perhaps for future reference! Rachel found him somewhat restless tonight - while I was at the Police Choir Practice - but, sensibly, let him wander while she got on with her work. I do not think we are important in Peter's world. I do not think there are many inhabitants in his world, but - and it is a big But - it is our responsibility to guard and protect his world for him. I hope we are doing this by keeping him at this current level of contentment. The reduction in stress and hassle for Peter has an interesting spin-off for those of us trying to care for him. The spin-off is that life now appears to be approaching normality. By this I think I mean that whatever is going on is now accepted as normal within these four walls. This being so, then we should all find that our own stress levels have been reduced. Of course, it may be that some of us may have adjusted the parameters of what may be regarded as normal in order to fit our own situations. Whatever the reason, I shall continue to welcome and appreciate our current situation. We have been caught up in some situations which have been a great deal worse. So, let us award the day 9/10.

Wednesday May 28th 2008

Rising time 1.35 pm.

Peter has had a very good day today. He has been smiling and tidying his box of books. Debi came today and expressed some concern with regard to Peter's muscle tone! I felt it only fair to say that his muscle tone seemed adequate to his needs. In fact, when one considers the amount of time he spends in walking round the house and the number of tea towels he gathers together and then folds up, it may well be that his muscle tone is outstandingly good. He is, after all, still upstanding! I may not add muscle tone to my list of points to consider. Today's ranking is 9/10. We are on a very good run at the moment.

Thursday May 29th 2008

Rising time 1.50 pm.

Something very interesting happened this afternoon. I have already mentioned that I am trying to give Peter his breakfast in bed, as I sense that he is then rather more willing and able to start the dressing process and, on occasion, to finish it himself. Well, this morning I took the tray upstairs, placed it on the chair next to the chest of drawers and gave Peter his medication from the small teaspoon. I went downstairs to finish sorting out Joe's lunch and then went upstairs to give Peter his tray. Imagine my surprise when I went into the bedroom and found Peter kneeling on the floor by the chair and trying to eat his cereal using the small tea-spoon. I had left the dessert spoon downstairs but Peter had solved the problem by using the only tool available - apart from his hands, of course. I was impressed by this evidence of brain activity - and can only assume that lining up the cutlery on a regular basis brings its own reward. I persuaded Peter to sit on the side of the bed and I then went for a more appropriate spoon. Kneeling down will have toned some muscles, as will the frequent bending action of picking up a huge number of leaves from the garden. The day has been warm and sunny. An ideal day for harvesting leaves. He filled his pocket with leaves and looked very pleased with his work. I shall award the day a ranking of 9/10 - especially deserved when I consider how much easier the ends of the evenings have been. Peter still seems to be more accepting of help in undressing. It is absolutely essential to hide each item of clothing immediately it has been taken off, otherwise he looks to put the clothing back on the body.

Sunday June 1st 2008

Rising time 2.05 pm - following breakfast.

June has made a rather wet entrance, but there is room for improvement. We have had a very good start to the day, which makes me wonder exactly where we are on the developmental scale of this disease. The current situation is very manageable and can almost be regarded as normal - whatever that really means!

I am wondering whether one's muscle tone is affected by spending long periods of time sitting scrunched up in a chair, as opposed to relaxing comfortably in a bed which has been equipped with an astonishingly comfortable memory foam mattress enhancer. I do not wish to become too obsessed with muscle tone - particularly as it has never before appeared in any of life's equations - but I do find myself wondering why on earth it has now become an issue, albeit a small issue. I fully appreciate the potential dangers of excessive sloth but I suspect the carpets in our house will wear out long before the residents' muscle tone. The whole idea has left me feeling more than a little exhausted so, at 11.55pm, I shall go for a seven mile ride on my excellent exercise bicycle, before bringing this day, which ranks as 9/10, to a happy conclusion.

Wednesday June 4th 2008

Rising time 1.50 pm - following breakfast.

I have been trying to engage Peter in some, any, sort of conversation, because I read, yesterday, that people with dementia in care homes seldom have more than two minutes of conversation three times a day with any member of staff. This has been condemned as disgraceful. I cannot argue with that but I am somewhat concerned about its implication for this care home. As the only member of staff I can honestly say that my one patient receives substantially more than this, but, I am no nearer solving the problem of how to engage in the conversation. Perhaps I am the only one who is failing in this respect, as people who come to the house and manage to catch sight of Peter, always say how bright and alert he is looking. How odd it is that, when I look again for this bright and alert quality, I so seldom find it. Unless, like beauty, it is all in the eye of the beholder. Ah well, with or without meaningful conversation, I am proud to rank the day as 9/10 – to be shared by all.

Friday June 6th 2008

Rising time 2.05 pm.

Peter was reluctant to get up after having eaten his breakfast, preferring rather to get back into bed and continue sleeping, or at least do some more relaxing.

Having closed my eyes to blips yesterday, I have to mention that the collapse of Thursday evening was truly spectacular. A true ranking would have descended into negative numbers - unless, of course, one was measuring how long it was possible for one pyjama-clad person to investigate the upstairs rooms of the house. One should bear in mind that these rooms are not explored during the daytime wanderings, because Peter does not venture upstairs. Consequently, I think he must have been quite bowled over by what he discovered last night. Even though I ended up taking out all the bulbs, except the bathroom and toilet bulbs, he still managed to explore in the dark. We had almost one and a half hours of knocking on doors, calling out "Hello!" and emptying the drawers. When I could no longer endure the excitement I instructed him to get into bed, close his eyes and go to sleep. This he eventually managed to do.

Peter's day has been good and the ranking stands at 8/10 - at present. He has improved his muscle tone and has also been more vocal than usual. I still fail to understand much of it but can guess at the remainder...

Friday June 13th 2008

Rising time 1.15 pm.

There is something vaguely unreal about life in this house. Peter appears to be very quiet, relaxed and quiescent, yet I am feeling more and more certain that some significant change has taken place within his brain. He does not make any sense at all of anything I say - even when I use my best miming skills. It used to be possible to attract him to the dining table by showing him his plate of dinner on a tray. Now he just looks, smiles, nods and carries on looking at his book. I am loath to serve his dinner on a tray. It is reasonably acceptable for him to have his breakfast sitting on the edge of the bed, but I am not certain that he needs to sit in a chair in the Study eating his dinner from a tray. I shall award the day a ranking of 8/10.

Saturday June 14th 2008

Rising time 2.25 pm.

It should have been rather earlier as Peter had his breakfast tray soon after 1.15 pm. I heard him go into the bathroom, whereupon I darted upstairs and made the bed. I stayed long enough to help him with his vest and then went downstairs. The weather was so tempting that I went out and started work on trimming the Rosa Rugosa hedge. When I popped back inside to check on Peter's dressing skills I found him fast asleep in the freshly made bed. This seemed to set the tone for the rest of the day. Peter's level of comprehension seems at an all-time low. He has enjoyed gathering up the ivy leaves, which are in great abundance following the earlier trim. The leaves are carefully gathered together, examined and then hidden in a dark corner of the garden. He then collects up more leaves and repeats the operation. While doing this he also discovered where I had hidden the remote control for the garage door and the front door keys. I keep these items outside so that I am in no danger of being locked out of the house. At least, that is what I thought. Today proved another example of my foolishness because, having found these two items, Peter gathered them up and went into the house. Oh yes, you are quite right, he did indeed close the front door. The garage door was already closed. It took me over half an hour to make contact with the jailer of what was to be an open-air prison. He could not respond to the doorbell or the door knocker or to my repeated calls through the letterbox. Eventually he came out of hiding and I spotted him, through the Music room window, folding up the tea towels. I could also spot the remote control and the keys neatly lined up next to the kettle!! I knocked, carefully and firmly, on the window to try and attract his attention. There was a remarkable lack of response for several minutes. When he eventually heard my knocking he turned round, waved and beamed at me in a kindly fashion before turning back to his folding. At last he was able to understand my dramatic gesticulations and made his very slow way to the front door. He was also able to open it and hold it wide enough for me to pass through. I shall have to forgo the easy routine I had established and hide a single front door key elsewhere. The day deserves a ranking of 8/10.

Thursday June 19th 2008

Rising time 1.25 pm.

In case you were wondering about any changes at the end of the day, I must hasten to assure you that the pantomime described in Stage One is precisely what we are experiencing at this exact time. Peter still has very little idea about the whys and wherefores of getting ready for a bath; consequently it takes an hour to complete the ritual. With that in mind it is still very important to look carefully for any positive factors which might present themselves. So, while I am looking, I shall award the day 8/10.

Friday June 20th 2008

Rising time 1.10 pm.

Peter is noticeably calm and placid these days. He is also unaware, as far as I know, that he is having bouts of bladder incontinence. I am monitoring the situation - we seem to do a lot of this - to try and work out whether:
a) he is aware of the urge and does not respond quickly enough;
b) he sometimes forgets how to respond;
c) perhaps he does not notice the urge and therefore cannot respond;
d) perhaps he has a problem with his clothing. I feel this is not

likely to be the answer - although I may be quite wrong - as he does not appear to have any difficulty with his clothing when weeing in the garden! The day itself deserves 8/10.

Friday June 27th 2008

Rising time 12.55 pm.

One thing I have noticed, over the last few days, is that when I come into the house, perhaps after collecting the children or running some errand, there is no response to my 'Hallo.' In fact Peter does not seem to notice my presence until I am standing in front of him. It may be that he does not hear me, or even that he does not register the meaning of the *Hallo*. Of course, it may be that he chooses to ignore me! Now, that would be interesting. My more serious observation would be that he associates sight *with* sound rather more easily than sight *or* sound. Another interesting development is that he is spending a lot of his reading time looking at books without pictures. The current one is *Our Mutual Friend* by Charles Dickens. The page is seldom turned and I do wonder exactly what he is making of the printed word. His world may be very small but he is certainly kept very busy with straightening things, lining things up, moving his books, hiding leaves and measuring out quantities of water in assorted vessels. He frequently bends down to straighten the small mat by the front door and is still trying to arrange the beanbags into shapes he regards as pleasing. All in all he has some arduous responsibilities - for which he deserves 9/10. Bedtime is still between 12.30 and 1.45 am, which is rather late, but it suits our domestic arrangements so we should not be concerned.

Saturday June 28th 2008

Rising time 1.25 pm.

Life on this particular plateau seems astonishingly easy. I am still wondering when that proverbial bubble will burst, but it may be that the bubble is un-burstable! Peter has been very busy with his many responsibilities and has been very helpful in drying up the dinner plates. One very good, and somewhat unexpected, change in response has helped to tackle a new problem. As Peter does not seem to be able to understand little instructions like 'Stand up, please,' or 'Sit down, please,' he needs to be helped to do those things. Until very recently he has found any sort of physical assistance very upsetting and totally unacceptable. Now, for reasons I cannot begin to fathom, he is accepting of a hand under the elbow, or the taking of his hand to lead him to the table, or another room, or wherever he needs to be. As long as the assistance is not sudden or jerky - and as long as he can see what is happening - he seems able to co-operate. Even getting ready for bed is less stressful. So I take pleasure in ranking the day as 9/10 - and allowing myself the luxury of a measure of contentment.

Sunday June 29th 2008

Rising time 1.15 pm.

We have enjoyed another straightforward start to the day and a calm and peaceful continuation of the day, although excitement and lively discussion do not feature in the daily routine. I am happy to say that Peter continues to busy himself with the lining up, etc., and has enjoyed looking at a newly discovered book on Gothic Art. He seems to me to be leading a happy life - and definitely prefers that happy life to be a quiet life. Well, who is going to argue about the appeal of a Quiet Life? I am certainly all in favour of such a thing! I think another 9/10 is well deserved.

Chapter Two - In which we face up to more problems

Monday June 30th 2008

Rising time 1.20 pm.

I happened to ask Amber this afternoon if she had noticed that Granddad did not seem to respond when we came into the house. If we called he did not answer, but, if we called and he saw us, then he would respond in some way. Amber said that, now it had been mentioned, she had actually seen that it was true. She went into another room and then came back to where I was still standing. "Well, Grandma," she said, "I think I know why he does that. If he hears, but does not see us, then he does not think he has to answer, but, if he hears and sees, then he thinks that it is important and he has to answer." I thought this a very good and carefully considered opinion for an eleven year old child, so, on that happy note, I shall rank the day as 8/10 and run the bath.

Thursday July 3rd 2008

Rising time 1.00 pm.

Today has been exceptionally good. Peter had his breakfast, decided to dress himself, without any help, and then to come downstairs and start the day. He has been co-operative, settled and busy. Consequently the ranking has been restored to 8/10. The difference in the last two days has been truly remarkable. I have not been able to think of any reason for yesterday's behaviour. Something odd must have been going on in his brain because, although happy to line things up and restore order in the toy box, he was not able to co-operate with anybody in the house. Neither did he wish to have any contact with any of the five people who visited. Of course he might have been overwhelmed by numbers. The day had started in a less than friendly way and had shown little improvement. Today is different and augurs well for a good mark!

There was another interesting event today. Fr. Petty, from Holy Family, came at 6.15 this evening to bring Holy Communion to Peter. Peter recognised his clerical collar and started to finger his own neck and tie. He did not seem to know Fr. Petty but he beamed at him and appeared pleased. At the beginning of the short service he followed the priest in making the sign of the cross - correctly - but was not able to join in with the words of the Confession or the Lord's Prayer. He made the sign of the cross after the Blessing and was very interested to see Fr. Petty sitting down in the other armchair. He smiled and nodded frequently during the following ten minutes, and then stretched across in order to clasp Fr. Petty's hand and shake it vigorously. I am very happy to say that Fr. Petty was very understanding and responsive to Peter. As he said, on his departure, "You never know what is going on in the brain, so be ready for anything, everything or nothing." One cannot find much to argue about with that observation, but the further loss of almost an entire lifetime's practice and devotion is only too painfully obvious. Peter really did not seem to have any idea of what was going on, but that is not really desperately important. The collar and the cross are still there in the brain. It is now midnight I shall try and end the day.

July 4th 2008

Rising time - another day for not rising!

Breakfast at 1.15 pm; dinner at 5.20 pm; coffee at 8.00 pm.

How shall I rank this non-day for Peter? If he has enjoyed it as much as I have, then it is a very high-ranking day and fully deserving of a spectacular 9/10 award. Well done.

July 7th 2008

Rising time 4.10 pm.

Although Peter ate his breakfast at 12.55 pm he managed to get back into an already made bed - obviously when I was not looking too closely. He seemed to fall into a very sound sleep in a very short space of time. He maintained this sleeping pattern whenever I went into the bedroom until, in the end, he tired of having to retrieve the duvet from the floor each time I took it off the bed! He then spent over half an hour putting on his clothes and eventually made his way downstairs. The children went home soon after six o'clock, which was the signal for Peter to start a serious marching routine. The routine included the back garden - when the rain permitted - the downstairs rooms and, by way of a change, the upstairs rooms. This is unusual because Peter tends not to climb upstairs until bedtime. However, I would always like to encourage healthy exercise, particularly as it has such a positive influence on muscle tone. When not toning his muscles, Peter has spent some time examining a leaflet on redundant churches, which he collected on one of his visits, at the end of the last century, to a church in Suffolk. He has spent a lot of time vocalising but I have not understood very much. I was able to work out what he was trying to say when he tried to ask me where I lived - and when I would be going back there. This does not result in a great conversation, but it can last for some little while. Drinking seems to be more of a problem. Peter does not finish his drinks and needs to be encouraged a lot of the time. It is a good thing that he still enjoys going to the tap, in the kitchen or bathroom, and drinking water - hot or cold - straight from the tap. It is interesting, considering the number of vessels into which he measures water, that he prefers to hold his mouth to the tap, as opposed to filling a glass with water to drink. Perhaps he thinks he is at school and drinking water from the water fountain. It is really time today came to an end but the chances of that happening seem somewhat remote. Things are still positive and, as far as the day is concerned, 6/10 feels about right.

Tuesday July 8th 2008

Rising time 7.15 pm. Hard to credit, but absolutely true!

Maureen, from the Continence Team, visited today. I had expressed an interest in meeting one of the team and Debi arranged for Peter to attend the clinic. This was not quite what I had in mind, as the prospect of getting Peter sufficiently organised to attend the clinic and then to be able to co-operate, seemed way beyond my capabilities. So, I changed the venue to our house, only to find that Peter had decided that today would be his day for staying in bed. Maureen arrived at 1.30 pm and proved to be a very pleasant, sensible and well-informed lady. We chatted for some ten or so minutes and then went up to see Peter. He was very quiet and did not feel able to co-operate at all, preferring to hide under the duvet and pretend to be asleep. Maureen quickly got the message and decided against doing anything at all. So we continued our chat downstairs - and I found it both interesting and informative. There are one or two factors we can consider and use whatever support seems appropriate whenever it seems necessary. From my point of view I have been able to pick Maureen's brains, access a catalogue of continence aids and ask several questions. I am left feeling that, for some reason, the whole subject of continence has been well and truly researched and many very sound practical measures have been developed - and made accessible for everybody facing any such problem. We shall see how it all works out. So, at one hour to midnight, Peter is wearing a blue shirt, pyjama trousers, his smart jacket and a pair of black socks. The day, which could so easily have become a non-event, can tip the scales at

9/10. Bedtime could be some time off. . . I hope it is before 2 o'clock.

Wednesday July 9th 2008

Rising time 6.20 pm.

Astonishing as this time may seem I have to say that Peter is more alert and co-operative if he gets up and dresses later in the afternoon - or even the early evening. There are obvious drawbacks to this sort of time-keeping but, at the moment, the advantages slightly outweigh the disadvantages. It is now 6.30 pm and he has already completed the destruction of one Fruit-shoot bottle - while trying to gain access - and has started on the folding routine. Rachel may have something to say.

> "Dad has 'talked' non-stop for 45 minutes. Mostly about the castle leaflet he is holding. There are odd words and phrases which give the impression he is loosely connected with what I am saying. Most impressive has been, "Did you ever seen about this one here?" Interesting how the verb tenses have gone, and definitely more dysfluent than I have heard in a long time. He looks worried tonight, not exactly switched on, but aware of things being wrong somehow. He is troubled by me, his tie, almost anything and his frequent sighs get louder if I do not answer him immediately.

> "Dad sat down at 9.30 after a busy evening peeling the tin foil from the coffee jar. He did pick up the leaflet on Kidwelly castle, look at it carefully and say "Kidwelly."

> "No idea where to put his cup; it almost went in the useful box. We have compromised on the mantle-piece, though this is not ideal given the long distance, tremor and almost missing the chair when he sits down again. I was reading tonight about another caregiver who bases her care on what

enables her to sleep with as little disturbance as possible. Like you, she had reasoned that if the person can't recognise things in the daylight, a light left on at night isn't suddenly going to create understanding.

"It is very difficult to switch off from the wandering and sorting while it is in full flight. I suspect I am listening for signs of problems, while not wanting to interfere with his train of actions if they are bringing pleasure or calm."

Thank you, Rachel, for these very helpful observations. The day has been very short but I feel that a ranking of 6/10 is fully justified - if only for his pronunciation of 'Kidwelly.'

Thursday July 10th 2008

Rising time 5.45 pm.

Unless I state otherwise Peter will be having his dinner - on a lap-tray - while sitting, tidily, on the edge of the bed. Breakfast will have been at 12.45 pm.

Once again Peter has been rather more alert and definitely a little more co-operative. Tonight I stripped the bed and then helped him to put on his vest. Having completed that task I left him to try and sort out the rest of the dressing. It has taken almost fifty minutes but he has come down with most of his clothes on the right part of his body and also in the correct order. He has obviously resisted the temptation to sort out the correctly re-ordered clothes and re-arrange them. That surely deserves a bonus point in the final reckoning! I wonder if Peter ever feels the appalling tedium and isolation which accompanies this cruel illness. I hope not, because where would he find refuge? At least I can go and sing or play the piano or even find a job of work I have conveniently forgotten. Peter is still looking at the leaflet on Kidwelly

Castle and seems to be enjoying the view. He suddenly looks very small and tired sitting in his chair. Perhaps he needs more sleep during the day? The day deserves 8/10 but some of us deserve rather more and will undoubtedly receive a merit of some sort.

Saturday July 12th 2008

Rising time 3.25 pm - this was much nearer to what we have come to expect - and can manage!

Exactly what has caused this return to what has become normality is hard to work out. Peter was in bed and asleep by 1.00 am so he should have had a chance to catch up on his sleep. But he also managed to dress himself today, so that is a very good bonus. I am running out of ideas to keep the focus on my record-keeping. It may have reached its natural conclusion, in which case I shall maintain a diary for our own use. It is not that nothing happens during the day, it is rather that there is such a repetition of activities - like the usual list of lining up, measuring, folding, etc., etc. - that nothing new is emerging. Perhaps if I suspend operations for a while I shall see some hidden excitement, or even some hitherto unnoticed facet of the illness. Whatever the outcome it is still essential to Keep Going, as the day is worth 8/10.

There is a definite change taking place, which I shall try and make sense of over the next few days and weeks. The change actually concerns what seems to me to be happening with the autism in Peter's life. As Peter becomes more deeply immersed in Alzheimer's so he seems to be losing some of the damage caused by autism. It may seem strange to use the word damage in this context, nevertheless it is, I feel, the correct word in this situation.

Friday July 18th 2008

Rising time 1.10 pm.

The standard of folding is now at a phenomenal level. If ever we needed proof of the old maxim 'Practice makes Perfect' we have it, here, in Peter's great interest in sorting and ordering those items some of us have chosen to disregard or ignore. The kitchen surfaces look almost manicured! But the most important feature of all this activity is the peace and calm it brings to Peter. There is no doubt in my mind that this is much more beneficial to his wellbeing than any therapy or activity anyone could have thought of. The muscle-tone of arms, legs, fingers and wrists, has to be of a very high order - comparatively speaking and taking genetic factors into consideration. I shall award the day 9/10.

Chapter Three - While the cat's away

Saturday July 19th 2008

Rising time 1.25 pm.

Rachel is on duty/guard while I am away for two days and one night, so I do hope she has a peaceful time. If the current practice is anything to go by I shall not be anticipating any major problems. Peter is so peaceful now it is hard to remember how appalling life was when he was in the grip of the demons of depression and terror. Well, it is not hard to remember, of course, but such memories only serve to make us grateful for what we now have. In anticipation of an exciting journey to the South I shall award the day 9/10 - and hope Rachel can match the score - while finding time to relax! I shall leave the all-important Care Plan and look forward to your observations, suggestions, advice, in fact anything else you might care to add, Rachel.

Sunday July 20th 2008

CARE PLAN for the period Sunday June 20th 2008 to Monday June 21st 2008

1.

On arrival at the house look in the kitchen to see whether or not Dad has eaten his breakfast. I will have left it set out on the table. If it is still there, place all the items on the lap-tray - the one with the blue teapot design - and carry it up stairs.

Place the tray on the black chair and draw the curtains. Say *Hello* and ask Dad if he would like his breakfast. This is a rhetorical question.

Give him his glasses which you will find on top of the chest of drawers - unless he has already found them. If he is wearing them, all well and good, if not, he may have hidden them under his pillow or secreted them in the top pocket of his pyjama top. Alternatively they may be lurking on the floor or in the bed. Do not worry about them as they serve no useful purpose. He can see perfectly well without them - unless he is driving the car. . .

Give him the tablets, from the teaspoon, and hand him the glass of water. Say, *"Swallow the tablets."*

Place the coffee cup, containing the hot coffee you made earlier, on the coaster on the chest of drawers. When Dad has swallowed his tablets pour the remains of the cold water into the hot coffee, to make the drink drinkable!

Pour the milk on the cereal and place the tray on Dad's lap. The only things on the tray will be the bowl of cereal and the dessert spoon.

Leave the room, taking the empty jug, teaspoon and empty glass downstairs with you.

2.

When you hear Dad go into the bathroom you will be able to run upstairs and make the bed. Place his clothes on top of the bedspread so that he can see his clothes in a line. Working from left to right: pants, socks, vest, space for Dad to sit down, then the blue shirt.

Go downstairs and allow at least twenty minutes before you go back and see if he has made any progress. He may well be half-dressed, so congratulate him, remove the tray etc., and go back downstairs.

When he comes downstairs, give him his toothbrush, remove the bowl from the sink and, using your best sign language, indicate that he should put the brush in his mouth and clean his teeth. Rinse out the sink as appropriate.

Take the razor, press the button on the side and hand the razor to Dad. Again help him to realise that he has to shave his chin. Afterwards, take the razor and hold it under running water. Then press the other button - to release the guard and cutter. Pull up the cutters and rinse under the tap. Rinse all three parts under the tap and place on the windowsill to dry off.

Make another cup of lukewarm coffee. Find a lovely apple, place it in a dish and carry it into the Study, together with the coffee - and leading Dad in whichever way you can manage!

Leave or stay as you choose.

3.

At around 5.30 pm, Dad would enjoy some dinner. Heat the dinner in the microwave and place the plate on the table. I generally serve the dinner at a *reasonably* hot temperature. If he is in the kitchen while you are getting the food ready you will find yourself feeling a little annoyed by essential items being removed from under your nose. I advise you to keep him in the Study until you are ready.

Offer the tablets, as marked, with a glass of water before he picks up his knife and fork.

Do not have the yoghurt on show as he will try and eat it or pour it over the dinner. Keep it as a lovely surprise until after he has finished his dinner.

Make a cup of coffee and let him drink it in the kitchen.

If you wash up some of the crockery and cutlery he will enjoy drying things and lining them up. He may also enjoy putting his hands in the washing up water and making the cuffs of his jacket wet! Not to be encouraged.

Stay or leave as you choose.

4.

Whenever suits you, and any time after 10.00 pm, you can give him the last of the tablets, as marked, with a glass of water. He likes a cup of coffee as well, but he rarely drinks much of it. I am sure you will do better, but do not worry as his fluid intake is reasonable.

5. Bedtime routine. For information only.

If Dad yawns or points his finger to the ceiling, I would change the date on the calendar and make some fatuous remarks about going to run the bath and get ready for bed.

Run a bath anyway and put in the bubble bath - in case he forgets to wash. This seldom happens.

Put the toothpaste on the upstairs toothbrush and place on the washbasin so that it is visible.

Turn on the light in the small bedroom.

The lights need to be on in the bathroom and the toilet. There is no light on the landing or in the bedroom. *BUT,* there is a small lamp by my side of the bed which should be switched on when you go to remove the bedspread and fold the duvet across the bed. Fold it across so that the whole of Dad's side is uncovered and mine is still covered - this time with two layers. Always try and anticipate a flash of inspiration on his part. Do bear in mind that he may be fooling us all and could be perfectly capable of doing all these things - if only his brain cells would let him!

It may be a good idea to place his blue pyjamas on the bed, as you did with his clothes in the morning, in case he decides to undress and get straight into bed. I have never known him do this before, but you never know what may happen today.

If he gets as far as the bathroom, and actually gets into the bath, it is important to remove the basket with any clothing in - I generally put it out of sight in one of the rooms – as he will put on anything he sees. I generally place his watch on the windowsill and give it back to him when he has dressed. Sometimes he needs help in fastening it on his wrist.

When he is in the bath hang the red pyjamas on the door-handle of the airing cupboard.

He can get out of the bath, dry and dress himself on his own.

He should clean his teeth and then he can be guided into the right room and be helped into bed. He usually needs to be told to put his legs up on the bed, then you can cover him up. He will need to have found his watch.

Turn off the light by my side of the bed.

6.

I always leave the light on in the toilet and put the chain on the front door.

The rest of the day is yours. But do remember to put the beanbag against your bedroom door so that Dad does not find out that the light switch works. He would be so pleased that he would have to spend the rest of the night clicking it on and off.

Monday July 21st 2008

7.

Before you go to work please will you set out the already measured breakfast cereal, etc., on the place mat on the table. This is in case Dad comes down at any time and then he can eat it.

Please place his clothes, in order, on top of the chest of drawers.

I shall leave out a plate of Shaper biscuits, a chocolate muffin and a lovely apple, which he can also have at any time.

8.

Extra Duties.

Please check on the state of the toilets at regular intervals.

J-Cloths and suitable Spray Bleach can be found near both toilets.

Make sure you have in your possession, at all times, the key to the back door and the remote control for the garage door. This is in case Dad chains or locks the door while he is on his incessant rounds and you find yourself locked out.

Please enjoy your stay and leave the premises as you would hope to find them!

Joe and I will leave Ash at 11.15 am precisely and will keep you posted, entertained and suitably informed at regular intervals. . !

Rachel's Comments and Observations.

"Sunday July 20th 2008

"Rising time began at 12.15 pm; breakfast on tray; one attempt to return to bed; no help required with dressing; declined afternoon cake but drank his coffee.

"He was very shocked to see me when I returned to give him his dinner, but then was very happy to see my car in the drive. There was the usual round of tidying up and lining up. All drinks were drunk today. He seemed to become more agitated between 5 pm and 7 pm when I was sitting with him in the Study, so I went into the other room and watched *A Secret Garden* on the television.

"There were repeated attempts to escape. I think he knew that something was 'wrong.' He seemed very pleased to see my car in the drive. He did seem to ask to go outside but, as it was not in the Care-plan, I could not permit it.

"He enjoyed looking at the paper and then found a book, called *Roman Italy*, which he then studied during the evening.

"Bath routine started at 10.10 pm and he was in bed with the light off at 10.45 pm.

"Got up twice during the night for the toilet and a wander round. He did not go downstairs, neither did he attempt to hurdle over the beanbag.

"Monday 8.00 am

"He was sleeping soundly when I left to go to work. I returned and served breakfast, on the tray, at 12.30 pm. He started getting dressed without a prompt and was downstairs at 1.40 pm. He scratched his chin and indicated that he wanted to shave. I went back to work and left him in good order."

Monday 4.30pm

Joe and I returned from our trip to the South at 4.30pm and found our arrival greeted by a very slight nod of the head, a little smile and the immortal words, "Ah, mmm." Everything is in perfect order, with Peter looking in equally perfect condition. It would appear to have been a very good and positive experience. So my grateful thanks go to Rachel, Stephen and Amber for making the whole thing possible, but mainly to Rachel for everything that she has done so cheerfully and generously. Today ranks as 10/10.

Wednesday July 23rd 2008

Rising time 1.10 pm.

Today has been very good and Peter has been in a very good frame of mind. He has, however, spent much of the day checking up on exactly how many people he can find in the house. I think that when there is a change in the routine and another person, such as Rachel, comes into the house - even if it is only for a short while - he does not actually register in his mind that, when that person leaves, at the end of the visit, then that person is no longer in the house. If two or three people visit then two or three people are still in the house, in Peter's mind, long after they have physically left the house. I went to the last Police Choir meeting for this season and left Rachel in charge. Peter spent *most* of the time sitting in the chair, and then searched the house for the best part of two hours after she had gone home. The day ranks as 8/10.

Thursday July 24th 2008

Rising time 1.25 pm.

The day has been spent marching, folding, sorting, lining up and challenging every single thing I have tried to do. He must be searching for a veritable army of people in this small house. I can only hope he was not too disappointed in what he found. 5/10.

Friday July 25th 2008

Rising time 12.45 pm.

Today has been a day of great frustration and annoyance - for me! For some inexplicable reason Peter has felt the need to try and sort through all my music, drop it on the floor and then try and put it out of sight. I ended up going upstairs with the paper - and the crossword - in order to control my anger. Perhaps one should not be too surprised at such reactions following thirty-six hours of normality, laughter and conversation - at any time during those hours, and not just when family members visit! What would we do without family members? Do remember to treasure your own family, bearing in mind that they are part of a bigger one. Another feature of the day has been an almost incessant flow of conversation, which would, I am sure, be very important and interesting - if only I could begin to make some sense of it all. Even *some* of it would be good. Debi, visited this morning. I rather think some of the thinking is a little bit of a challenge. It was, however, interesting to note her reactions to the Care Plan and Rachel's response to it. I was not convinced that she felt it was the sort of programme one could attempt to impose on a care worker. Perhaps it would be too demanding. My first thought was that the consequences of not adhering to such a simple, straightforward and *tested* routine, might well be rather more demanding! What say you? The day can have 6/10.

Chapter Four - Making sense of what we have

Thursday July 31st 2008

Rising time 7.25 am. Yes, that is exactly right. I was deeply shocked!

Peter spent last night in the chair in the Study and decided to wake up early. He was eating his breakfast soon after 7.30 am. It was all somewhat un-nerving. His mood has been very odd today. Although he has slept for most of the morning he definitely seems a little bit different. I have a theory about this sort of change, which I will try and develop later on. It is worth reflecting on the implications of this behaviour and sorting out in my mind exactly what I am trying to think and/or say. So, let us have a ranking of 5/10 - for the sake of generosity.

Perhaps now would be a good point at which to reflect on what seems to have been achieved thus far.

Peter's Physical State.

Peter is rather more frail and I would say that this frailty has increased over the last ten or so days. He finds it more difficult to get out of his chair and to stand up. Interestingly he seems to find the whole enterprise rather amusing, because he never fails to laugh while he is trying to get up. He keeps on smiling while he totters across the room and finds the door against which to lean his shoulder. I am trying to keep the weight on him by giving him a few extra calories from time to time.

Hearing.

His hearing is rather worse now, but there is still the possibility that he is opting not to hear certain things. Having said that, he no longer tries to reach the telephone when it rings; neither does he respond to the doorbell. The odd thing is that I would not have expected him to respond to those sounds in the normal course of events, but he has been opting to hear them. So, what are we to make of that? He does not understand when I tell him that his dinner is ready - even if I am standing in front of him with his dinner on a tray. He looks at me as if I have taken leave of my senses, when I start, at bedtime, to engage in the conversation necessary to persuade him to get out of the chair, leave the Study and climb up the stairs. There must be something in the sequence of words because he generally finds it highly amusing. I find it slightly less amusing.

Dressing and Undressing.

Getting undressed is very unpredictable. Sometimes it follows a reasonable pattern - by that I mean he is co-operative - while on other occasions he becomes very annoyed. If I leave him and carry on cycling round the Pyrenees he has been known to try and wrestle with his shoelaces. If he can manage to do something, anything, about his shoes, he seems more willing to let me finish the job. Whoever thought of teaching children to secure their shoes with double knots, or even bows? Sometimes he has tied them with three knots or bows. My heart has been known to sink while I struggle in the dark to wrestle with those thin black strings. Velcro seems such a sensible form of fastening. For the general benefit of the entire nation it may be appropriate for traditional shoe laces to be issued with a Health and Safety warning!

Eating and Drinking.

Peter eats all his food and seems to enjoy it. He rarely indicates that he is hungry and will, even after eating a substantial dinner, eat any food I might have forgotten to put away. This leads me to think that he is not registering fullness or hunger. The same applies to drinking, although I have noticed that he would rather drink someone else's drink than his own!

Continence.

Praise be! He still has it.

Hobbies.

Lining up, measuring water into cups, jugs and dishes, folding cloths and picking up small items from the floor still take up a significant part of his day. He is particularly fond of collecting leaves and blades of grass. These are placed in his pocket and then arranged, in a tidy line, on the dining table.

Conversation.

There is a reasonable amount of conversation but not the sort which can be understood by anybody else. Of course there is the occasional exception. A *Morse* DVD was on over the weekend and when Peter came into the room, en route to the toilet, he stood and looked at the screen. As he did so, one of the Oxford Colleges came into view. Peter looked, beamed and announced, perfectly clearly, "Ah, Oxford." He still expresses opinions on the pages of his books and is always pleased to hear a supporting response to whatever he is expressing. I would love to know just what I was agreeing to or with!

Spirituality.

There was a most interesting situation when Fr. Cavey - parish priest and a colleague of almost thirty years - came with the Sacrament of Holy Communion. Peter's response was quite unlike his response when Fr. Petty came. On that occasion, a mere four weeks ago, he seemed to respond to the clerical collar and he was also able to make the sign of the cross. With Fr. Cavey's visit it was different. He did not make any initial response and seemed to be puzzled by his presence in the Study. There was no attempt to make the sign of the cross, or to say any words of any prayer. He was very pleased to shake Fr. Cavey's hand afterwards, beam and smile and then bid him farewell. This may well be indicative of how far Peter is regressing.

My hypothesis, for such it is, leads me to think that periods of markedly unco-operative and irritable behaviour coincide with a regression in Peter's mental state. He always seems to be more childlike afterwards and does not regain any of the lost ground. I think there is a very young human being inside that frail body now. William, at five, seems very grown up by comparison. My last reminder is that I do not think Peter's failure to hear is optional in the generally accepted sense of the word. It seems to be rather more of a case of the brain opting out on a physical level rather than the *individual* choosing to opt out.

Let us have 8/10 for perseverance. Now that I read it through I can see no new thought or discovery. What next? Any idea?

Sunday August 3rd 2008

Rising time 1.55 pm. I was late back from Church, having been unexpectedly delayed.

Peter has been busily absorbed in his sorting and folding. He seems to me to be taking some degree of pride in his work. The muscle tone in his legs must be more than satisfactory, as he has now been attracted by the videos and CDs, and spends some considerable time on his knees while he tries to line up the boxes. This is rather more challenging than cloths, because he cannot change their individual shapes in order to fit them into a space of his choosing! He accepts the challenge with good grace. Lining up, folding and marching has broken all records today. Peter ought to feel totally exhausted, but I can see little evidence of that. The day deserves 7/10.

My atlas has flipped open to show France in all its shapely splendour. Looking at Orleans has reminded me of a wonderful photograph Peter took of one of its most famous Boulevards. This, in turn, has given me the idea to re-examine the beginning of what might have been a great Boulevard in Manchester. The bike calls, loudly.

I am now on the bike and heading in a northerly direction in an attempt to locate Ashton New Road as it leaves Beswick and opens out into Ancoats. I remember, most clearly, that the year was 1995 and Manchester was doing its best to put in an impressive bid to host the Commonwealth Games, due to be held in the UK In 2002. A great deal of money was being spent in developing various parts of the city and a major road-widening had begun, in order to create an impressive entrance to the city. This included widening Ashton New Road and also providing a great number of posts, which were destined to hold beautiful hanging baskets of colourful flowers and leaves. At the appropriate time - that is when the inspection of the improvements was due, prior to the bid being submitted - beautiful hanging baskets, at a cost of £25 each, were placed on the black and gold brackets on the posts. I must mention that the posts were the height of lampposts.

My route to the School, where I was Head Teacher, took me along this newly widened road twice each day. Within a week I started to notice gaps in the basket display. Each day I realised that there were fewer and fewer baskets on their brackets. It was not long before I was offered several hanging baskets for a mere £3.50p each. Yes, my top junior boys, my eleven year old boys, were at it again. It was not too difficult for an adult to arrange for the removal of the baskets, provided there were enough young boys to find homes for them. I resisted the temptation to buy. But before long, an enraged City Council had ordered the complete removal of the last few baskets and had arranged for their discreet disposal. The black and gold brackets are still on the posts - perhaps in readiness for the next time. If asked, I would recommend the miniature - but very tough - spiny berberis as an excellent plant for our particular climate.

Ah well. . . back to Denton.

Saturday August 9th 2008

Rising time 1.25 pm.

What a wonderful gift we have in *hindsight*. If only we could access it *before* the event we might make more sense of what we do in life! Grasping the gift of hindsight I can see, quite clearly, all the signals which were pointing to a further decline in Peter's condition. The struggle involved in getting undressed - plus the fact that his pants and trousers were soaking wet after visiting the toilet. I am using the word *visiting* because if I say he went *into* the toilet it sounds as though he climbed into the lavatory pan, and I have no evidence to support such a thought. If I say he went *to* the toilet then it suggests that the floor is not included in the operation and it was, most definitely, included in this particular operation. Perhaps the solution is to have a *bathroom* and then we can add another dimension to the situation. It was very evident that Peter did not understand anything that was going on. This can be accepted, but it becomes almost impossible to do anything to help things along when the person not understanding cannot make sense of what he is being encouraged to do. I only have one such person to cope with - and all the time in the world as it is the only *work* that comes my way now - so imagine what it must be like to have a whole roomful of such confusion. Such chaos in need of being pulled into some sort of order. On second thoughts, do not try to imagine it. When I went to get Peter up this morning I found him fast asleep in bed - minus his pyjama trousers. They were neatly folded on the beautiful, elegant escritoire - wet through. But, Peter had understood enough of that situation not to stay in his wet pyjamas - so some brain cells are working, and fortunately the flood was confined to the floor of the bathroom – and the ever-faithful mop and bucket were both on hand to deal with the situation – without comment, complaint, protestation or reaction of any sort!

Dressing was a very lengthy process, mainly because I tried to let him manage some of it on his own. It is still very important to let him take as much time as he needs: to ensure some little remnant of independence. As I have already mentioned, time is on our side! Today is Peter's birthday and he is seventy-four years old. The celebration has not been very noticeable, mainly because he has slept through the day.

I shall award 10/10 as recognition of today's birthday - and the promise of free TV viewing, to be enjoyed by both of us, when he reaches his seventy-fifth birthday.

One point I omitted yesterday was the fact that Peter became disorientated again and tried to wee in the garden. When that attempt was thwarted he corrected his mistake and tried again - in the corner of the kitchen next to the fridge! This attempt failed and, third time lucky, we located the correct room. Puddles are the order of the day now so we need to make sure there is an ample supply of Flash with bleach, and appropriate floor cloths. I am still of the opinion that this does not count as the sort of incontinence which would necessitate the introduction of continence pads. This a path from which there would be no turning back, so, for the time being, I will have to raise the level of supervision when he is wandering about. 9/10 today. It might be worth noting that there was an inexplicable bout of fist flailing at bedtime. Something was not exactly as Peter had in mind. Never mind. Better luck tomorrow.

Wednesday August 13th 2008

Rising time 1.25 pm.

The effort of eating breakfast, getting dressed and coming downstairs must have been a very exhausting experience as Peter went straight into the Study, sat in his chair and went to sleep for fifty-five minutes! After that he was able to undertake his usual task of sorting and folding. He had calmed down last night and was able to co-operate at bedtime - although he could not get himself into bed in a sensible fashion. A 'sensible fashion' means that, once you are sitting on the edge of the bed, your head is closer to the head or pillow end and so your feet will be nearer to the foot of the bed. A fashion devoid of sense means that you are sitting at the foot of the bed, refusing to move and wondering why your head is not able to reach the pillow. The resolution of this problem takes some time - and can cause an increase in hysterical tendencies on the part of the person trying to change the manoeuvre. The best cure for such a situation is a seven-mile ride on the exercise bike.

Sunday August 17th 2008

Rising time 2.05 pm.

It is worth commenting on an unusual, possibly even original, piece of behaviour which I noted last night. The getting ready for bed procedure could have been described as within normal limits, so I was a little taken aback when I went into the bathroom to help Peter. He was washing his hands, most vigorously, with a white substance which did not seem to be providing very much in the way of lather. When I subjected the substance to the famous Nose Test - this never fails - I was able to identify the white substance as Tooth Paste. Good for teeth but less than impressive as a hand wash. The problem is that toothpaste is, by definition, a rather sticky substance which does not rinse off too easily. The whole experience seemed to interest Peter so, in the interests of economy at this stretched time, I shall keep it, the tube, out of sight. With all the tallying, folding, lining up and sorting that has gone for the last two hours and seven minutes I am reminded of that poem by Henry Reed - *The Naming of Parts*. I remember particularly the lines:-

> "Today we have naming of parts,
> Yesterday we had daily cleaning.
> Tomorrow we shall have what to do after firing,
> But today we have naming of parts."

Of course, Henry Reed was writing of a war situation and the parts mentioned were parts of a gun. Nevertheless, the words keep ringing through my head, as there is a definite method in what Peter is doing with his grouping and re-grouping. Naturally, one would not wish to forget other important lines, such as, 'of which we know nothing' - which pretty well sums up what we are about! 9/10 would be a fair score, I think.

Monday August 18th 2008

Rising time 1.45 pm.

Put not your trust in Princes, nor yet in the previous day's ranking! There have been many bonuses today, but, I have to admit, the last five hours have not been included amongst them. Peter, for some reason, has lost the proverbial plot. The greatest problem seemed to be when I sat in the Study re-threading my beads. Perhaps he only recognises me in the Study when I am attached to the laptop. For whatever reason, he found it necessary to stand over me and to move each bead at the precise moment I was trying to thread it. I have managed to thread the *beads* but *I* am somewhat un-threaded by the whole enterprise.

I shall have to apply my mind to a possible alternative as far as the bath is concerned. At present Peter just manages to get in and out of the bath but, due to his physical frailty, each time looks as though the effort of getting his legs over the edge and into the bath is becoming greater and greater. I was wondering about a walk-in-bath, but, after due consideration and reference to Rachel's experience and knowledge, I see that the demand on Peter would be way beyond his ability to comprehend what was required of him. So many aids are excellent if people have well-developed brains and can understand how they work. It is no wonder that people can be so frightened of hoists, which come and scoop them up and then transport them to they know not where. Imagine Peter trying to sit in and try and operate a stair lift! No, I can't imagine it either. I cannot rank the day as more than 2/10. This could be further reduced if I hear the front door being opened and closed many more times. I wonder what I shall learn when hindsight kicks in - perhaps in the not too distant future! It is now 11.20 pm and Peter has collected a book entitled *Britain from the Air* and is sitting quietly and happily in the chair. He appears to have forgotten his obsession with doors, hangings and curtains. I shall relent and award the day a ranking of 5/10.

Friday August 22nd 2008

Rising time - there was no such time today.

In some respects today will feature as a non-day event. Despite the monthly visit of Debi, the CPN, Peter preferred to spend the day, or the greater part of it, either feigning sleep or else actively engaged in sleeping. It took some little while for Peter to wake up for long enough to eat his breakfast - at 1.45 pm. He clutched the duvet to his chest and refused to entertain any notion of putting on his vest, pants and shirt. After what I considered to be a reasonable length of time, namely before the urge to kill overtook my brain, I abandoned all thought of trying to establish a normal, for us, day! He had put his socks on by 5.30 pm and was wandering around in his pyjamas. I quickly heated up his dinner and managed to persuade him to sit at the table and eat his food. This he did. The evening was spent upstairs, in semi-darkness, and involved a lot of sorting of clothes, papers and toys. He then went back to bed. I failed to give him his medication, which may explain why he was able to sleep so well during the night. At midnight I had a bath and went to sleep in the children's room. How does one rank a non-day? Perhaps 1/10 - for being in the right part of the house at dinnertime. It *could* be 2/10 as there have been no puddles today!

Sunday August 24th 2008

Rising time 3.15 pm - for no good or particular reason that I could quite discover.

I have realised that, apart from any other factor, the main benefit of keeping to the form of a daily diary is that it enables me to end the day. This may sound somewhat odd but this is the way it seems to work. It is sometimes rather easier to recall the more trying elements in the day and this can result in a negative feel to whatever has gone on. Gone on! What a quaint little saying. To continue. By noting the positive, as well as the negative, features and ascribing a suitable score to the day as a whole, one is left with the realisation that all has not been negative. Some moments may have been funny, worthwhile or even successful: these will balance the tedious and wearisome nonsense that can sometimes seem to cloud the day. It is then possible to rank the day and put a full stop to that particular period of twenty-four hours. Tomorrow can then be a new day and the previous day put in its rightful place. I am now wondering what Ted Hughes, the poet, had in mind when he said,

"Today I can see that in front of me stands yesterday."

That could be a rather sad and depressing thought. How much better it is to put a full stop at the end of each day and file it away - for future reference if desired! So, after all that, I am going to put a full stop after a ranking of 5/10 and look ahead to whatever tomorrow brings.

Peter is less connected than ever and looks as though he is part of another world. When busy he is certainly involved in something - I do hope it has a purpose. Let those who think such thoughts are fanciful please note that constant exposure to this condition, for both the patient and the carer, teaches us something we do not always have occasion to notice in the more conventional world. As we know, it has to be *lived* to be *believed*. I still struggle to believe it. In fact, I frequently do not believe it. Perhaps we should have some sort of *Mission Statement for Carers* who do not believe the evidence of their own eyes.

Thursday August 28th 2008

Rising time 1.00 pm

Yes, I realise it sounds incredible but there it is! Peter ate his breakfast soon after one o'clock but then climbed back into bed - even though I had stripped the bed in order to wash the bedding. He managed to retrieve the duvet, which was resting quietly on the floor, arrange the pillow and get into bed in order to go back to sleep. At six o'clock I took Peter's dinner upstairs so that he could eat it when he was ready. He has been studying *Bleak House*, sideways, upside down, right way up, even closed, since half past six. But, since then, I have had occasion to realise and fully appreciate the great value of all those hours he has spent in developing his folding skills. I had spent a little while making some cotton-jersey cases for some blocks of memory foam, which I thought, might prove to be useful to use in Peter's chair in the Study. As he was busy trying to investigate the workings of the sewing machine, while I was actually using it, I decided that he should apply his mind, in a very practical way, to the job in hand. The job was to fit each of the eight blocks into its appropriate case. At this stage I had managed to make three cases, so there was a need to increase production and speed of production. To my amazement he was not only delighted to have such an exciting job, but he was also very, very, good at fitting each piece of memory foam into its new stretchy case. He spent no less than one hour and eight minutes on joining together eight cases and eight pieces of foam.

I suspect that Debi would describe this as an example of Perseveration. I have already mentioned this condition in an earlier section and it relates to an activity, such as walking around, scratching skin, or rubbing at pieces of material. It is supposed that, unless the patient is discouraged from such persistent behaviour, he or she may well continue with the activity for a very prolonged period of time. Perhaps there is a simpler explanation. Suppose the person has an increased ability to concentrate on certain activities. Perhaps that person has not become trapped in the activity. Perhaps that person is actually concentrating on something that is fitting in with whatever process is going on in the brain at that particular moment, or moments, or hours! Peter was very happy with his work and took great pride in smoothing out all the many wrinkles in the cases. It was a job well done and has gone some way to achieving a ranking of 9/10 for the day - which is good by any standards.

Friday August 29th 2008

Rising time 1.35 pm

Peter was most co-operative as far as dressing was concerned and did not protest when I cut his toenails. While I was doing his nails I gave him his tie to try and fasten - as a distraction. Imagine my surprise when he said, very clearly, "What do there?" while pointing at his tie. That was as near as he has come to making me understand a sensible question. I showed him how to fasten his tie and he, beaming broadly, generously allowed me not only to finish fastening the tie but also to finish his nails. You cannot ask for much more than that! The day continued in a pleasant and calm way. Again he did not register the existence of the children, but seemed very happy to gather twenty-five crab apples from under the tree and to load them into his jacket pockets. Once back in the kitchen he arranged them, most carefully, in five groups of five apples. I wonder exactly what we should make of that. Cerebral activity of a high order comes to mind. There have been no puddles for eight days so perhaps that is a problem which has been set to one side. A ranking of 8/10 is fully justified.

Sunday August 31st 2008

Rising time 2.35 pm

Today started off in a very encouraging way. Peter had his breakfast and co-operated with the dressing routine. I left him, to answer the door-bell, and returned to find him well on the way to finishing dressing. It was only two hours later that I discovered that he was still wearing his pyjama trousers under his suit trousers. It was not a problem for him so, I concluded, there was no reason for there to be a problem for anyone else - least of all, me! He had folded his clean underpants most carefully and placed them under his pillow. Having spent much of the time between 3 and 5 o'clock sitting down he had difficulty in agreeing to eat his dinner at the dining table. He had it on a tray while sitting in the beanbag. That was the easy part of the day. One or two challenges had been prepared for the evening. Things like persisting in trying to open the mortise-locked front door, and emptying the contents of my diary onto the table with the intention of folding all pieces of paper - all essential in various odd ways - and lining them up with the cutlery. He has started putting the cutlery away in the tea-towel drawer. This is rather odd because he has to find, and then open, the drawer to do this. The normal place for the cutlery is clearly visible and has been in the same place for the last thirteen years. He has enjoyed strolling round the garden and gathering up many crab apples. He still gathers, polishes, and places them in his coat pocket, and then takes them out to eat at odd intervals. This sequence of events seems satisfying. I am having to be on constant guard as far as the water taps are concerned. I have seen him turn the tap on, stand there seemingly watching the water as it comes through the tap - and then walking away without making any attempt to turn off the tap. Of course, if I intervene and remind him that he has to turn off the tap, he has no idea what I am meaning. When I demonstrate the art of tap-turning he has been known to beam at me and then clap both hands in a cheerful fashion. This may be fun for some, but I am mindful of the fact that we are on metered water! I think I shall have the taps changed and new ones fitted which will turn off automatically after a set number of seconds. This will reduce the threat of flooding, if I do not happen to be on strict supervision duty at any particular time. It is now eleven o'clock and Peter has settled down for the evening. I do hope it is not a long one! The day should rank as 7/10 - possibly a little more if this calm interlude lasts until bedtime.

Wednesday September 3rd 2008

Rising time - a very co-operative 1.25 pm.

It has been a very good day indeed, with Peter busying himself with folding, sorting newspapers and straightening cutlery. Rachel has very kindly started the Wednesday supervision duties, while I go to the Police Choir practice. She did say he had been very busy while she was here, but she did not mention the wanton vandalism of the aerosol can of Raid Fly and Wasp Killer - with thirty-three and one third per cent extra and at no extra cost. This is the second known attack on this aerosol can. The last attack responded to careful persuasion and the nozzle agreed to be re-united with the main can. This attack, however, has been carried out in a meticulous and possibly calculated way so that First Aid has proved to be totally ineffective. I have to point out that, with Rachel's own admission, this act of vandalism was unsupervised at all levels - which raises some questions with regard to the attacker. It is now half past eleven and Peter, obviously overcome by the activities of the day, has had a bath and is now in bed. I cannot believe this and shall have to have a bath and go to bed - in case I wake up and find it has all been a dream. The minimum ranking for today has to be 10/10.

Thursday September 4th 2008

Rising time 1.45 pm.

It is now ten thirty pm and Peter has been wandering around since Rachel collected Joe just before seven o'clock. I know that both Joe and Amber have found the almost silent creeping around a somewhat daunting experience. I shall have to try and think of a way of reducing their exposure to this element of Peter's behaviour. It is far from easy for them and neither is it desirable for young people of almost twelve and sixteen to have to worry about what Peter is going to do next. When they come back from school they should be unloading burdens - as well as bags - not picking up new ones. I shall have to apply the grey cells and try and come up with a solution. It would make sense to ask the young people concerned what might be helpful and useful for them. A youthful approach to a problem can sometimes yield surprisingly successful solutions - even one solution would be most welcome. The day deserves 7/10!

Monday September 8th 2008

Rising time 2.25 pm

Peter has had a very good day today despite its rather late beginning. I think he must have exhausted himself in the garden yesterday and found it necessary to catch up on his sleep. Rather sound advice I think. One thing has become increasingly apparent of late and that is the real distrust of the TV set. I have mentioned before that Peter does not like the television to be on, particularly if there is anything remotely busy on the screen. I think I have also mentioned that he thinks anything of a military nature is actually going on in the room. This does rather reduce the appeal of the TV. I have been trying to watch some of the Proms this week, but it has not been an outstanding success. One might say that the success rate had been totally marginalised. Not only does he think that the screen characters are real but he also thinks that the cast and set, of any situation, have taken root in the corner of the room. This is particularly disconcerting when he is trying to tell them to go away - or at least I think that is what he is trying to do. They may be guests in our room but they are not at all welcome. The relief is huge when I turn off the television and the visitors - and their surroundings - disappear from the scene. It is a pity because I would have liked to watch the Proms. Whichever level Peter has landed on, at the moment, is a very relaxed and comfortable level for everyone concerned. We could stay on this level indefinitely and manage without the television. I shall have to work out what I am going to do about the flu jab which is currently on offer. The logistics involved in organising Peter on a trip to the surgery are quite extraordinary - particularly when the only reward is a needle being pressed into his arm. Which thing he will neither appreciate nor understand. But I do have a few days in which to consider the options. The day, thus far, ranks as a good 9/10.

Thursday September 11th 2008

Rising time 4.35 pm.

Despite the late rising hour, Peter has been very tired today and opted to get ready for bed soon after a quarter to eleven. I have, however, discovered a very interesting fact with regard to the bedtime routine. It is much easier all round if, when I help Peter to undress ready for his bath, we actually put ourselves in the bathroom. Until a few days ago, the undressing process would start in the bedroom, where jacket, tie, jersey, shirt and trousers would be taken off. We would then move into the bathroom before taking off vest, pants and socks. Teeth would be cleaned and then Peter would get into the bath. Now, however, there have been more problems over *what* is happening and *why* it is happening. This can be very stressful - and annoying - for both people involved. A much simpler way round the problem - so far - is for me to run the bath and then take Peter into the bathroom. I then help him with his jacket and toss it out onto the landing. I then unfasten the shoes and toss those onto the landing. The same then applies to the tie, trousers and the jersey, but care must be taken that these items are tossed out quickly and unobtrusively because, if they are spotted, then they become the most desirable things in the world and a big fuss follows if Peter cannot have them. I have now achieved a high level of discreet skill, which talent may be in great demand one day. The remaining items of clothing will be placed in the laundry basket in the bathroom. Provided Peter can see the water in the bath, complete with bubbles, and I keep mentioning the phrase 'the bath is ready,' then we can make impressive progress. I still leave him to get out of the bath on his own and to dry himself, after a fashion, and to put on his pyjamas. I want him to do as much as possible for himself, and for as long as possible, as I have noticed that lost skills remain lost and he has lost more than is in any way reasonable. He has been very busy indeed today and the towels have been tastefully arranged over the cooker and on all work surfaces. I shall not attempt to cook. Instead I shall award the day 8/10.

Saturday September 13th 2008

Rising time 2.10 pm.

Today has been a day of unsurpassed excellence - or words to that effect. Perhaps we have both learnt lessons from yesterday's experience. For whatever reason Peter has been very much more reasonable in his behaviour today. I shall not have to worry that he is developing the dreaded *Attitude Problem*. Just imagine a gentleman of seventy-four with an attitude problem. I cannot begin to imagine such a situation without wishing to collapse into somewhat hysterical laughter. Of course it is always possible that *I* had, or even have, the attitude problem. Ah well, we shall see what tomorrow brings. The day deserves a ranking of 10/10.

Tuesday September 23rd 2008

Rising time 4.35 pm.

Although Peter was up and dressed rather earlier than yesterday he does not appear to have suffered any harm. One thing I have noticed over the last few days is that he is having a significant problem in sitting down on the very safe swivel chair in the bathroom. There seem to be two problems.

1. What is it and what is it for?

2. How to sit down on the chair.

Once we agree that Peter is going to sit on the recently purchased, highly desirable, shower/bath chair, he then goes through a protracted sequence, during which he looks at the chair, puts one hand on the bath, moves away from the chair, looks at it, leans towards it, tries to turn round while looking at it and then falls against the airing-cupboard door. The next sequence is the whole performance involved in trying to locate exactly where he should sit - if that is what is required. He seems far from convinced of the sense of that idea. But eventually, when I have had enough excitement, I help him to sit down - sometimes in the middle of the seat, by applying some gentle pressure - it can also be described as a very discreet push! My main concern here is that his sense of space seems wildly out of order. Perhaps the proximity to the wall and the airing cupboard is causing a problem. Who knows! I shall have to pursue this, but first I shall award the day a ranking of 9/10.

Wednesday September 24th 2008

Rising time 2.35 pm.

Rachel has come up with a bright idea over the chair problem. She is wondering if the fact that the chair is white - and so is a perfect match with the bath, the washbasin and the two painted doors - makes it more difficult for him to identify it as a chair. I shall follow her suggestion and place a coloured towel on the chair before Peter tries to sit on it. Another interesting, if slightly odd, happening was when I found Peter kneeling on the floor and trying to clean his teeth using the freshly run bath water - complete with foaming bubbles. Again Rachel was able to come up with a brainwave. Because the ten seconds worth of water from the newly purchased taps over the washbasin had come to an end, and, as Peter had not known, at that moment, how to get any more water, he used the water he could actually see. It all makes perfect sense and shows a cunning brain is still at work. I shall sign off with a ranking of 9/10 and a comment on the happy atmosphere in the home today. Peter has spent most of the time being happy and smiling, so something is working properly in this very odd existence.

Thursday September 25th 2008

Rising time 1.25 pm, but do not take this too seriously.

Today we discover that there are breath-stopping occasions in the unpredictable life of those persons in our situation. On Tuesday I mentioned the little matter of the chair in the bathroom. On Wednesday, following a professional consultation with our own NHS representative - namely Rachel - I prepared to ease Peter's dilemma with the identification of the afore-mentioned chair. This, you may recall, would consist of disguising the white chair as a blue chair. This would be achieved by draping a blue bath-towel over the white chair.

Ten minutes after midnight we went upstairs to start the bath/bed routine - and test out the success of the disguise. I am happy to be able to report that Peter was delighted to see a blue towel over the white chair and, with a beaming smile, sat smartly and confidently upon it. There was no sign of the previously mentioned routine, the one involving bending, leaning, lurching and finally half collapsing into the chair. Due to excellent muscle tone, which, although it has not been mentioned very much of late, is a dimension of life occupying the forefront of our minds, Peter has not only been able to sit comfortably but also to remain sitting. He was so thrilled with his achievement that he refused, most emphatically, to move out of the chair and most certainly not in order to take off his jacket. I eventually managed to relieve him of his shoes and jacket but that was the sum total of my success. The story appeared to finish as Peter left the bathroom and went into the toilet. I took the opportunity of getting in the bath. I then got into Amber's bed and listened, for some little while, to the cacophony of clicks from switches, thuds from doors and the sound of the drawers from the chest of drawers being emptied of their contents. The next surprise was the undeniable sound of feet, wearing shoes, going down the stairs. This struck me as interesting as it would appear that Peter's dexterity had been restored in some way. I then went to sleep. At twenty past five I was awakened by the sound of Peter going into the upstairs toilet. I wondered if he had been sleeping in bed but, on looking into the bedroom, I found the bed as I had left it - with the duvet turned back and the small lamp switched on. I quickly pulled the duvet straight and went downstairs to see how many lights were still on. The Study, hall and kitchen lights were on and Peter had obviously been busy sorting out the books in the Study. I turned off the lights and managed to get back into Amber's bed before Peter came out of the toilet. It was then very quiet. In darkness and silence I continued to listen to and try to interpret sounds of stray movements until I fell asleep. The alarm sounded at seven o'clock, so I got up and went to see what had been going on since half past five. Peter had obviously gone into the bedroom and drawn back the curtains. He had then taken off his jacket, tie, shirt, shoe, socks and trousers - they were all neatly folded and arranged on the chest of drawers. He had then got into bed, arranged himself tidily and comfortably - and gone to sleep - leaving me to marvel at such a, generally invisible, high level of skill.

Peter had his breakfast soon after half past twelve. You will not be surprised to find that, being asked to take off one vest and put on another - and then repeat the operation with his underpants - caused some confusion. It did not, however, result in a refusal to co-operate, and the day has continued in a very positive and cheerful way. Perhaps a ranking of 9/10 is justified as an acknowledgement of the successful practice of what might appear to be low cunning. The brain is a truly remarkable organ, so remember not to underestimate its potential.

Friday September 26th 2008

Rising time 3.45 pm.

Debi visited this morning and we had an opportunity to comment, very briefly, on a gap between the USA and the UK - as far as research is concerned. We seem to be stuck with the labels, mild, moderate and severe and very little guidance as to how and when such labels may be useful to the carer. We sometimes seem to work on the principle of least said, soonest mended - which, as we all know, is far from being the general norm.

However, it was an interesting meeting. Again the subject frequently escapes discussion but, as a result of the on-going assessment - on-going now for eleven months - we reached the joint conclusion that Peter was in the severe stage of Alzheimer's. I have asked Debi to investigate the scale and come up with some sort of idea. Not that any idea will make any difference, because as we all know, the effect of Alzheimer's on an individual is as unique as that individual. It is now eleven o'clock and, after a short but very sensible day, Peter has embarked on a mighty search for something which involves opening the front door and looking in the porch every few minutes. He has made seven searches so far, so I think we may be in for a silly hour or so. Until the silly hour started the day would have been worth 8/10.

Monday September 29th 2008

Rising time 2.35 pm.

I have just realised that tomorrow will see the recording of the eleventh month of Keeping Going. I can scarcely believe that there is such a comprehensive record of life in this house over that period. From my point of view it has been immensely useful, and of great value in getting to grips with the way Peter has been affected by Alzheimer's disease. It is also most interesting to see the way Peter's nature appears to have changed, in order for him to cope with the various stages. At the moment he is a most amiable, peaceful and seemingly contented person. Nothing happens to upset him and he obviously finds great comfort in his many attempts to create order in the tea-towel drawer. I find myself wondering whether this has any connection with the personality of the very young child - before the shackles of autism started dictating the many pitfalls he was to find in his struggle to fit into a society which puzzled him so very much. Alzheimer's would seem to have removed some of those shackles and provided him with a world in which he is at ease and with which he is contented. Days which cannot be ranked really reflect the vagaries of the carer as much as the challenges of the one receiving the care. I am in duty bound to rank the day as 9/10.

Tuesday September 30th 2008

Rising time 1.25 pm.

There is an element of excitement pending the arrival of the final month of recording our ability to Keep Going. It is most interesting to see the somewhat restricted way the activity has chosen to move. Nevertheless, it has been an important part of the coping strategies we, as a family, have adopted over these many months. Today has, in fact, been a very good day. Peter is very attracted by the plastic A4 pouches I use for some of my music. Unfortunately his interest lies in removing the sheets from the plastic. He has now discovered a green A4 ring binder - full of plastic-clad sheets of music. I shall have to keep an eye on what happens to it at the end of the evening, as he has developed a great talent for storing other people's possessions in secret places, known only to, but forgotten by, him. It is certainly occupying his brain in a useful way. So, for many reasons I shall award the day 10/10 and gold stars all round.

On a final note I must mention that, having spent time sorting out my music, Peter, who has never learnt to read music, has spent almost two hours studying the notes printed on the page. Is it a question of white on black or black on white - or neither of these possibilities?

I would like to leave the last words of this particular stage to Joe - Peter's sixteen year old grandson. Joe had been reflecting on the effects of Alzheimer's on his Granddad. I find the words and the pictures they evoke incredibly moving.

"The Forgotten Body

Unaware of what's before them,

Blind to what's behind,

Stripped of all emotion,

Lost on the inside.

Missed and mourned for dead,

Though well above their grave.

What is life without a mind?

Just a lost and lonely soul

Wandering high above its body."

Stage Three

Chapter One - Reviewing the situation

Sunday October 5th 2008

Rising time - before 1.45 pm.

Today has been most interesting in many respects. Before leaving for church I had taken Peter's breakfast upstairs on a tray. There was, as usual, a bowl of cereal, a jug of milk and a glass of water. This was in case Peter woke up and felt like eating some food. On my return I noted that the bedroom curtains were still firmly closed. I unpacked my music bag, set the dryer, and made two cups of coffee, before going upstairs to see if Peter had woken up. When I went into the bedroom I walked over to draw the curtains before I realised that Peter was not lying asleep in bed. He was actually sitting, in the dark, on the edge of the bed, looking at and holding onto one of his shoes. Having drawn the curtains I could now see that, not only had Peter poured the milk on his cereal and eaten it but he had also drunk the water from the glass, and then placed the glass back on the coaster I had placed on the top of the chest of drawers. That was a pleasant surprise in itself, but I was most impressed to see that Peter had put on most of his clothes - in the correct order and on the correct part of the body. He had yet to sort out the tie and shoes. All this had been achieved in the dark - unless he had drawn back the curtains, eaten his food and put on his clothes and then closed the curtains again. This does not seem very likely - even in our unlikely way of life! When I consider how he manages to wake up in the night, get out of bed and walk to the toilet, then walk into the bathroom, wash his hands and then come back and get into bed, all with only the benefit of one light in the toilet, I find myself amazed at what his brain can tell him to do without the need for any light. The Famous Automatic Pilot possesses a pleasingly high level of competence!

I really must note that, as far as home is concerned, Peter seems to be finding, and presenting, considerably fewer problems than over the last months. I feel that the reason may be found within the many words written over these months. We have, as a family, talked and pondered over many aspects of Peter's condition, with particular reference to the things he can and cannot accept and/or manage. I feel fairly confident that, because of the contemplation of these many and varied situations - and the act of writing about them - we have, in some way, made it possible to join Peter's needs with our family needs so that previous tensions have been eased. It may have taken the best part of a year to work this out, but I am increasingly convinced of the positive help that recording our experiences has been for all the people involved. It has been a most valuable learning experience - as well as an important means of family communication and understanding. So, in conclusion, I shall award the day 10/10 - a round of applause and a hearty pat on the back to everybody involved.

Thursday October 9th 2008

Rising time 3.55 pm.

This week could be the week to break all records. Peter has had an excellent day with nothing to cause distress or upset. One of the items for which I am exceedingly thankful is the white swivel bath chair. I have only just worked out exactly why it is so useful as far as helping Peter to undress is concerned. As it is set in the locked position - and so does not swivel around - Peter feels very safe and secure on it. Also the design means that the back and seat is moulded as one unit, but the arms are separate from the body of the chair. This is to accommodate the swivel, but, for our requirement, it means that there is much more actual arm room. This is very important when trying to negotiate the removal of jackets, jumpers, shirts and vest because all these items can be removed while the wearer is sitting down. When Peter is required to stand the chair arms provide the necessary support - and, with average luck and provided the belt has been unfastened and the waist band has been undone, then, when he stands up, the trousers should fall down round the knees. If he then collapses in a heap onto the chair, then it is very simple indeed to remove the trousers and socks - but do remember to remove the shoes first. I am absolutely delighted with it, even though I thought that charging the general public twice the amount that was charged to the NHS was outrageous. I am, however, happy to have it, regardless of cost.

The day deserves another 9/10.

Friday October 10th 2008

Rising time 12.35 pm.

I realised at half past two in the morning that Peter had not completed his daily quota of sorting and lining up. Somehow or other his concentration on developing muscle tone had slipped and here he was, at half past two in the morning, trying to sort and line up the contents of the top drawer of the chest of drawers. During the next two hours I put Peter back into bed no less than four times. The fact that he got out of bed within a few minutes gave me the clue that he was not understanding that I simply wanted him to lie down in bed, close his eyes and go to sleep - so that I could do the same. The drawer was not in need of this attention to its contents. In the end, once my poor brain had realised that I was on a losing wicket, I left Peter to wander round the house and line up whatever he wanted to line up. All I had to do was to pretend to be somewhere else. Anywhere else! At one point I felt a very cold hand on my face, but I pretended to be invisible and the hand went away. He must have been very cold but was obviously not registering the fact. This is usual for the disease but most unusual for Peter, who has never relished being anything other than pleasantly warm. I went back to sleep before Peter had finished his wanderings and his work, and was awakened by the sound of the telephone ringing. It was Joe ringing to ask me where his maths homework might be. It was a good job he rang because I might have gone on sleeping.

Unusually, only one light had been turned on and left on, and that was the Hall light. Perhaps Peter only went downstairs and did not conduct a full tour of the house. I do not know, as I was asleep at the time - I expect. As we must all try and learn from our mistakes I have decided which lesson I shall learn. Peter's level of exhaustion must not influence the time he gets up. It is so much easier for me if he stays sleeping in bed but, if it means that he spends time being busy in the middle of the night - and bedtime is very seldom before one o'clock - then it does not really make for an easy day. Not because of Peter's behaviour but because I find I feel somewhat weary. So, today I have made sure that he has had the opportunity to do plenty of work during the hours of daylight. This was not supposed to include slipping quietly out into the garden and then weeing in the corner. I shall just have to keep the back door locked unless I am on guard in the kitchen. This is a shame, but is, I think, necessary. The garden is very secluded but one never knows who might be peering through binoculars while making a study of the local wild life! The night deserves 1/10, but today has been redeemed and so a ranking of 8/10 seems reasonable. On reflection, I am not convinced that enough work has been done to ensure a quiet night. If Peter wakes up, and does not settle, I think I shall withdraw from the scene and leave him to his wanderings - wherever they take him.

Saturday October 11th 2008

Rising time 12 55 pm.

I have to report a great improvement of late. Until a few days ago Peter could never tolerate any distracting sound, e.g. Radio Three or Classic FM. Somehow the changing dynamics caused him great agitation. All music had to be played at the same volume. Unfortunately the great classical composers were unaware of this requirement. Consequently, Beethoven, Verdi and definitely Wagner have all disobeyed a cardinal rule. This has been a severe pain and grievance to me. But, over the last few days I have been able to sit in the Study, with the laptop on my knee and listen to Classic FM or Radio Three. The relief is unbelievable. My prison has suddenly been provided with escape routes - and how I am enjoying each and every one. This is exactly the sort of thing which enables one to continue in a reasonably balanced fashion. It may have something to do with hearing but, selfishly, I am not going to investigate too closely. If a clue presents itself to me I shall take note, otherwise I shall follow my own advice: leave well alone and ask no questions.

As we approach the final weeks of this Magnum Opus - my exaggeration is permitted, I trust - I am trying to work out what, if anything, has been achieved, by these many thousands of words. My natural feeling tends towards flippancy and, it may be that at the end, flippancy will take over, but, for today, I am going to try and look carefully at what might have emerged.

1. The first, and somewhat disconcerting, fact is the overwhelming number of times the pronoun *I* has been used. When one is supposed to be considering another person it is alarming to see how often one's ego appears to dominate. On the other hand, as a fully paid-up member of the Worldwide Carers' Association, it may be inevitable. It would be depressing to think that this had only served to give space for me to talk about myself. My mother often said to me, "Remember, Kathleen, do not talk about yourself." It would seem that I have totally ignored her undoubtedly sound advice. Perhaps you, who are so kindly and patiently reading this, will bear with my fall from grace - and learn from it.

2. As a fully paid-up member of the afore-mentioned Worldwide Carers' Association, one is required to *multi-task* but it is not essential to *omni-task*. Perhaps this is a new word which can be introduced into the vocabulary of those of us with an inflated ego. I am not claiming this distinction for myself, naturally. Modesty would forbid it. Naturally.

3. Perhaps the most important fact to emerge is the importance of spending just a second or two at the end of each day - or, if that is too horrid a time, choose a more agreeable second - and reflect on whether there has been anything in the day deserving of a tick rather than a cross. It is extraordinary how beneficial it can be to realise that not everything you have done has been wrong, silly or counter-productive. It may be that the person receiving your care has deserved a tick rather than a cross at some point during the day. Of course, there is always the chance that the Cared-for has more ticks than the carer. Should this happen, double your ticks until your total is greater. It will do you the world of good and improve your confidence in yourself and in how and what you are doing. You might even like to reflect upon this conundrum when relaxing - which you must do - with a (small) glass, dram, tot or piece of Thornton's chocolate.

4. The last point I am going to make today is that, as far as Alzheimer's disease is concerned and because it works/attacks in a slightly different way for each unique and individual person, it is crucial that the fully paid-up member of the Worldwide Carers' Association should find a way of caring that *works for the carer*. If it works for the carer then it will work - as far as is humanly possible - for the one being cared-for. Trust yourself and always take great care to follow your own advice as you are in control of the work. Listen to others, of course. Consider their advice carefully and, if it matches your own - or what you would have thought of, given time - then *follow it*.

I shall take a leaf out of my own book and award the day 10/10 and many ticks.

Tuesday October 14th 2008

Rising time - a very respectable 1.10 pm.

Peter has spent most of the afternoon in the Study - only emerging from time to time when he felt the need to fold up a few tea towels. I am constantly amazed at the order and tidiness I see in the kitchen. It may not be as I would have left it but, somehow, Peter manages to find new and exciting ways of arranging cloths and papers, cutlery and glasses, in designs worthy of display in the Tate Modern. On the strength of his co-operation and amiability, Peter and the day deserve a ranking of 10/10. It is well worth mentioning how much easier the bath routine has become. I put this down to the fact that Peter goes from the Study, straight upstairs and into the bathroom where he can see, immediately, the bath full of water and bubbles. He can generally manage to sit down on the swivel bath chair - in the locked position, you may recall - and seldom causes any problems as far as parting with his clothes is concerned. For my part, I am convinced that, as he can see the water in the bath, he has more confidence in what is going on. I would not say that he, necessarily, knows the individual stages of taking off his clothes - in fact he has been known to try and take off his socks while his shoes have been firmly attached to his feet - but the sight of the water seems to keep him focused on some sort of objective. If I am fooling myself, so be it. All I can say is that this routine seems to be stress-free for Peter and is, most definitely, physically much less demanding on my silly weak arms and hands. I was wondering if anything might present itself as a potential difficulty for Peter when actually getting into the bath.

I have come up with these observations. The close proximity of the washbasin to the bath means that there is a substantial support within very easy access to the bath. The grab rails on the side of the bath are also ideally placed - so, all the time Peter can raise one leg high enough to clear the height of the bath, he has maximum support for lowering himself into the bath and enjoying the experience. The wall with the radiator is near enough to the bath to provide additional support, should he manage to lose his balance, or move awkwardly when climbing out of the bath. Provided he pays great attention to his muscle tone I would expect him to be able to manage indefinitely - so here's hoping.

Wednesday 15th October 2008

Rising time - a very cunningly planned 1.35 pm.

Today has been another exceptionally calm and peaceful day. I do hope Rachel is able to share in it this evening and is not left to question my sense of honesty and justice!

> "I arrived at ten past eight only to be met by an empty Study. Dad appeared from the toilet some fifteen minutes later. He smiled broadly as he came into the kitchen, folded up some newspapers and then proceeded to wash his hands. He also tidied up my coffee cup and altered the arrangement of the biscuits, thus giving him some essential activity and the all-important input into his muscle tone. There is certainly a change of atmosphere in the house

as described in the events of the last few days. It is a much calmer and more peaceful place in which to be. Your increasing sense of optimism in your writing, Mother, must have permeated through the house. I do not think Dad has wanted to be in the Study with me tonight. I am disturbing his peace?"

Some persons do not know when they are well off, Rachel. I am glad you have been able to complete some work. I shall award the day 9/10.

Thursday October 16th 2008

Rising time 1.45pm - the day of the medication review.

"Today is the day we worried about yesterday, while tomorrow will be the day we are worrying about today."

The word *problem* can be fitted in wherever you feel appropriate - if you feel it to be appropriate and/or necessary.

At 6.15 pm we set off for the Surgery to see one of the doctors with regard to Peter's medication - I was looking for approval for a further twelve months on the same course of medication for Peter. We saw the doctor, who decided that it would be a good opportunity to take Peter's blood pressure, and also to arrange for the nurse to take some blood for a series of routine tests. She would be able to do this after she had given Peter his flu jab. Needless to say, the only person who had no idea of all these great plans was Peter - the subject of the investigation. Taking the blood pressure was a challenge in itself, because of the need to remove the jacket and roll up the sleeves of the shirt and the jersey. Some might have gone sporting their vests and short-sleeved summer shirts, but that is not the way Peter likes to do things. Of course, today would have to be the day he was wearing his shirt with the double set of buttons on the sleeve. He tolerated the taking of his blood pressure without flinching. There was the odd flinch as the band tightened round his arm, but I thought he coped very well indeed. I mentioned to the doctor that if we could take the blood sample while he had his jacket off and his sleeve rolled up, then that would make life easier all round. But, of course, the nurse would be responsible for that procedure and she functioned in another room. So, down with the sleeves, on with the jacket and back into the waiting room. Peter was not happy with the idea of sitting waiting, so, having been persuaded that it was not possible to walk into each of the consulting rooms, he decided that the thing he needed, above all things, was a drink of water. This is communicated in a routine of mime, which comes into play whenever we get into the car or reach an unrecognised place. It can be very tedious indeed. Today was no exception and provided only a mild level of interest to others.

After only a few minutes - which seemed like only a few hours - we were called in to see Julie, the nurse. She was very good with Peter and he shook her hand most warmly. Then, of course, we had to repeat the process with the jacket, then the jersey and finally the shirt. The flu jab was met with complete outrage, much squeaking, puffing and panting and pulling of the arm. It took two of us to hold on to the arm - and the syringe - while praising Peter for his patience and other sterling qualities. I was relieved to recall that the pneumonia jab had been given last year and, as it lasts a lifetime, would not have to be repeated.

The next excitement was the taking of blood. Although I am fairly certain that Peter had forgotten the sequence of the flu jab, he was still somewhat rather taken aback when the syringe went into his vein. He had been interested to have the mini-tourniquet round his arm and to see the vein standing out in his arm, but he was not prepared for yet another needle attack. Of course the blood took its time leaving the vein and I think it was absolutely miraculous that we managed to hold

Peter's attention long enough to let the syringe fill itself. After that process I had my flu jab and, naturally, displayed the restraint, courage and dignity one would expect from someone drawing the State Pension. Peter then shook hands with Nurse Julie and we came home.

Apart from sticking to me like the proverbial limpet, Peter has settled reasonably well. In fact he has now indicated that he wants to go up to have a bath and get into bed. So I shall stop and give the day 11/10 for courage, patience, good-humour, endurance and perseverance which, naturally enough, proves to have nothing whatsoever to do with the previously mentioned perseveration. I could grow accustomed to days like today - although we do not need the blood-letting!

Sunday October 19th 2008

Rising time 2.10 pm.

I am delighted to say that when Peter did get up to get dressed he was most co-operative and amenable. Pouring and measuring water into and out of a variety of jugs, cups, glasses and even an empty glass jar, have been the favoured activities today. When I consider the range of activities, limited, by some standards, but satisfying to Peter, the pattern that emerges is predictable and repetitive, so that the end of this month would seem to be a very appropriate point at which to finish this stage of the record-keeping. We have, most definitely, Kept Going and the overall pattern, which has emerged over the year, is clear and helpful - at least it is clear and helpful from my point of view. I shall hope to form some sort of conclusion which will stand on its own and allow whatever follows to have a separate and independent identity. It is not my plan to spend another year writing about the excitement of sorting and folding! Today will rank as 8/10.

Tuesday October 21st 2008

Rising time 1.10 pm.

I have been sent a booklet on *Dementia*. It is a beautifully produced document, with excellent pictures of gentle looking persons and a text in a large clear font. I am absolutely delighted with it. It has been beautifully thought out and put together. It is full of excellent and sound thinking and has, for me, been a really interesting and useful booklet. In seventy-nine pages it has managed to put down all the information it has taken me eleven and a half months and three A4 Ring binders of work to record. Nothing has been missed out. What it has done is to make me feel that we, as a family, are still achieving a good standard of support and care for Peter, while still, somehow, hanging on to our own individual identities. This has to be very important.

Wednesday October 22nd 2008

Rising time 2.20 pm.

This afternoon presented something of a challenge, as it was necessary for Peter to sit on the edge of the bed in order to eat his breakfast. Peter suddenly found that he did not know how to sit down. He walked round the bed, through the door, beamed and smiled, tried to pick up the cereal bowl and only managed to sit down in response to a measured push - on my part. During the course of the afternoon he helped himself to a small red apple, ate it and then walked around looking for somewhere to place the core. He did not respond to the idea of the rubbish bin.

As it was going to be a late evening Amber chose to have her dinner here and decided on pasta, beans and roast potato pieces. I had counted out eight small cubes of potato and left them in a dish just before putting them in the oven. I went into the garage with some cardboard and, on my return, noticed that Peter was busy trying to *tame* something in his mouth. Yes, you have guessed correctly. Having spotted a dish of *something* he took a piece and put it in his mouth. It was a frozen potato cube, which would have challenged most people. Peter persevered with the frozen cube until he had chewed it up and swallowed it. I tried to suggest that he take it out of his mouth and throw it in the bin, but he refused to be deprived of his nourishment. Whether it gave him any pleasure I cannot say, but I do think he showed great courage in the face of adversity. Also, I wonder if he was registering the fact that it was not only cold but also very hard. Amber thought the potato was delicious when hot and soft, so I might show Peter that there is another way of eating potato cubes. I am wondering if Peter is developing a light-fingered attitude to life. Perhaps a food safe might be an investment during these times of possible austerity. The entire evening has been spent in the kitchen - practising the usual skills to perfection. Let us award the day 9/10.

Sunday November 16th 2008

Rising time 1.05 pm.

Disgraceful. Never let it be said that Alzheimer's disease displaces Autism and becomes the dominant factor. This particular possessor of the Autistic brain is not relinquishing his internal *modus operandi* for anybody. No, we must accept that, in this case at least, autism is fully capable of jostling into a position of superiority. That being so I shall award the day 4/10 - mainly because of the total absorption of self. I know that is part of the condition and that I should accept it and get on with it. Well, tonight I must say that part of my condition does not wish to accept or to get on with it. My condition states, very clearly, that I am able to refuse to accept anyone else's condition at the expense of my own. Perhaps tomorrow will be different.

Chapter Two - More of the same

Tuesday December 2nd 2008

Rising time 1.05 pm.

Today has been a very interesting and, in some ways, an illuminating day. It really started with Molly. She was not fit to attend school, so we began planning one or two activities for the day, but then Peter started his wanderings. I decided that he had better eat his breakfast and get dressed. He ate the breakfast. I started the dressing and then Molly called. Peter heard her call and looked very perplexed. I finished posting him into his shirt and jersey, and then gave him his pants to put on his legs. I then took the tray out of the bedroom and went to see to Molly. After about twenty minutes I went back to see how Peter was getting on. He had managed to see to his pants but had started on the folding routine. Nothing in the drawer would escape. I asked him if he was all right, whereupon he glared - that is the correct word - and said, most clearly, "No! I am not here!" This comment, apart from being inaccurate, was a perfectly constructed sentence which would, in a different situation - e.g. the world of wizards and magic - have been a very useful and informative sentence. In a way it was informative to us as it enabled us to see that Peter is still capable of stringing some words together which could, in certain situations, be relevant and important. It is not always easy to find the correct response to someone who claims not to be where he appears to be. I took the easy way out and suggested that, when he came back, he might like to finish drinking the cup of coffee I had left for him on the chest of drawers. I was conscious of a hard stare as I left the bedroom and went downstairs, to discuss the finer details of one of the *Winnie the Pooh* stories Molly and I were enjoying together. After another half an hour Peter arrived downstairs in a reasonable condition and in an amiable frame of mind.

When we finally met up in the same room he seemed to be very relaxed and content. Perhaps he had finished all that he had set out to do. I shall, with relief, rank the day as 9/10. He is now asleep in the chair so the bath/bed routine may be prolonged.

Wednesday 3rd December 2008

Rising time 1.25 pm.

Here are Rachel's most helpful comments, written while I was enjoying myself at Brian Basan's Advent soiree.

> "Dad really does spend an awfully long time negotiating his exit from the bathroom after a wee. I think it must be all the turning around. Now, your comment about "Do you exist when you are not there - in Dad's world?" Well, it is, perhaps, back to object permanence. He no longer has that reliably, as a concept, so of course when you are out of sight you do not exist. Maybe he had been looking for himself in the drawers and, perhaps to his great surprise and disappointment, found that he was not there! I am alone in the Study, while his coffee is cooling nicely. Folding and pacing are in full swing.

> "When Molly and I were reading *The Milk is in the Oven* - a book for children about dementia, Molly was very clear, when we read some of the words other children had used to describe their feelings about their relative, that neither she nor William thought Granddad was scary. In the way and confused, yes, but scary, no.

> "I have made weak coffee just to make sure I am not

accused of leaving you with a stimulant filled person! He has had a very restless evening. Dad has cut his finger on something; haven't been able to work out on what, but possibly the razor. No plaster visible, but cold compress briefly applied. There has been much talk of going up, but then being distracted by the coffee jar, books, doormat etc. He has been opening the door more than I have seen him do for a while. Again, as with last week, I think Dad is not at all sure I should be here. He keeps trying to direct me somewhere and then shrugs, glowers and leaves. There was an interesting little jig that started with neck twitching, running on the spot, shrugging and then a brief round of applause. I didn't join in. "Oh you're here then," has been heard along with attempts to tidy all my things away. You are right. There are more words, Mother. I do not think more words signify Dad being in a happy place in his head. I think the words come out in desperation, to allay the confusion. When he is silent, I think he is happy; he is possibly so confused he does not have to worry about it. In fact tonight has been about aimless wandering, not productive sorting and measuring. Something has shifted. If we liken Dad's head to a snow scene globe (well mine is, so there is no reason why Dad should escape), then it has been shaken up and has settled with the grey cells firing differently again. His peace has been disturbed. I steal that line from someone with autism who describes talking, on the part of other people, as disturbing her peace. This can, sometimes, be true for us all.

"I suspect the odd aggressive incident is also a result of Dad's world being unsettled somehow, probably his internal world. I do not see it as a response to what is going on outside. He keeps on showing me his cut finger. Saying it is all better seems to work for the moment."

Thank you so much, Rachel. After a lovely evening I shall award you and the day 10/10.

Tuesday December 9th 2008

Rising time 1.20 pm.

There has definitely been some change in Peter's condition, but I am still not absolutely sure about its significance. He is still on the march and another thing I have noted is that, if I am in any room, for any reason, Peter immediately wants to stay in that room and sort it out. The interesting point is that he does not wish me to remain in that room with him. Consequently it is necessary for me to stop what I am doing and move out. I might add this does not cause a problem for me, as whatever I am doing is unlikely to be of national importance. Also it is easier to find some other activity which can be done without supervision. Peter has, somehow, managed to work out the mystery of the lever arch file. He is very occupied with removing his photographs from the file, inspecting them carefully and lining them up. I must check that they are returned to their rightful places. The day deserves 9/10.

Monday December 15th 2008

Rising time 2.10 pm.

Peter was agitated when he woke up and this continued throughout the day. It was, initially, reflected in marked and physical aggression when it was time to dress. He tried, with all the facial mannerisms, to engage in some sort of wrestling bout. Now I am not a wrestler by nature, neither do I know the rules, so I had to make up the rules as I went along. Rather than engage in complicated and possibly foolish-looking poses, I chose to stand firm - or even firmly - and, without uttering a single syllable, fix my assailant with the proverbial hard stare. I also realised that, in this battle for supremacy, I also held what might be described as the trump card, namely strength. I have the greater physical strength - so take note! The afternoon proved to be rather tedious in that Peter is obviously feeling threatened by his surroundings. It has been becoming increasingly evident that Peter is finding it difficult to cope with the sight of any cutlery or crockery in the washing up bowl. Perhaps he thinks it is his responsibility to sort and clear any muddle. I shall reflect on this idea tomorrow and credit today with 5/10 - even though 3/10 feels more reasonable.

Tuesday December 16th 2008

Rising time 1.15 pm.

Today has seen a great improvement in all areas. I am still feeling more and more certain that Peter likes to be the architect of his own disorder. If he sees something out of alignment, or can see a way of improving on an existing arrangement, then he is very happy to spend a considerable length of time sorting out a perceived improvement. But, if he finds himself confronted by dishes needing to be washed, or books in a tidy pile or clothes in need of folding, then he seems to fall victim to attacks of panic and/or fear. I shall rank the day as 8/10.

Wednesday December 17th 2008

Rising time 1.20 pm.

Peter's behaviour has been very calm today. I am, however, certain that there has been a further *slip down* in his condition. He has been unable to settle to anything, preferring to stand under my feet, watch whatever I am doing and make many totally incomprehensible comments. He is also gesticulating a lot. Most of the time he seems to be imitating a windmill in full sail. That normally applies to a ship, but I am sure it could apply to Peter's windmill. He is also trying to swing his arms in an alarming way, as he tries to clap his hands first in front and then at the back. Today I have had to stop trying to understand the communication system. It may be clearer tomorrow. So, on that cheerful note I shall rank the day as 8/10 - strictly for calmness. It would be a different figure if I happened to be ranking him on the effect on other family members. They themselves are deserving of a generous accolade.

Sunday December 21st 2008

Rising time 1.00 pm.

This was deliberately early because Joe and I were going to The Bridgewater Hall for the Halle Orchestra's and the Halle Choir's Annual Carol Concert. I was anxious to have everything in place by the time Rachel came to take over the reins until we returned. It was particularly important as there had been a significant blip last night. I went up to run the bath and get everything ready for the bedtime routine - which amounts to putting toothpaste on the brush and finding the clean pyjamas. When I went downstairs to begin the process of encouraging Peter to get up from his chair and climb the stairs, I found Peter already standing in the hall. He climbed the stairs in a willing enough manner but was decidedly odd when I pointed him in the direction of the toilet. I left him in the bathroom while I went downstairs to turn off the lights and check that the front door had been locked. When I went into the utility room I was met by an enormous puddle on the floor. I immediately decided to invest in a new mop and bucket, which would be kept in the utility room ready for emergencies. I then mopped, washed and disinfected the floor before going upstairs. Peter was decidedly unco-operative - which was not surprising considering that his clothes were wet through. Having said that, I am still certain that he was not aware of wetness, *per se*, but he was aware of something he did not like. This made him aggressive. By the time I had managed to help him take off his jacket, jersey, tie and shirt, he refused, point blank, to part company with his trousers and underpants. In fact I left him in the bathroom, still punching the air - because he could not get at me - and locked myself in the toilet. I waited for about five minutes, by which time I would have expected him to have got over the initial frustration which had caused the aggression. On going into the bathroom I found that he had rescued his shirt, tie etc. etc. from the laundry basket and put them, more or less, back on his body. I started the routine again as though nothing had happened. Peter was subdued and I had the feeling that he was trying to express regret for something he thought he might have done. I chose not to tell him what it was. Bath time and bedtime continued in a reasonable way and Peter eventually got into bed. I got in the bath and locked the door - which was a good idea as he soon got out of bed and started his wanderings. On finding the bathroom door locked and hearing no answer to his "Hallo, Hallo" - no joke intended - he went back to bed. By the time I was ready to get into bed he was fast asleep, and slept very soundly.

On our return from a truly wonderful concert, which Joe and I enjoyed immensely, I found Rachel looking rather wan - partly due to her heavy cold. She had also been met by an enormous puddle in the utility room. She was successful in her mopping, washing and disinfecting procedures, but was concerned that she had failed to persuade Peter to change his wet clothes. There would never have been any chance of this happening, because he would have needed to know what he was supposed to do and, more importantly, why he would be required to do it. This is way beyond his ability to comprehend. The idea of changing the style of trousers, into easy-fasten or stretch-waisted trousers is not, in my opinion, a reasonable option at the moment. Having spent most of his life dealing with a zip and several buttons, the process of learning to apply a new technique, when already being bombarded with messages from brain to bladder, is not going to meet with any level of success. The logic seems very obvious to me, so I shall have to try and interpret a few more messages. What an exciting life we shall lead! Despite the blip I am going to rank the day as 8/10 because Peter has been very calm and controlled this evening and is still struggling to master the wilfulness of the lever arch file.

Wednesday December 31st 2008

Rising time 1.45 pm.

We shall be able to note the passing of the year 2008 as an achievement. But we must all move on and I am hoping that Peter can be absorbed and catered for in a successful way in 2009. We shall, I know, as a family team, be doing our very best to juggle any new demands with characteristic good humour - and grind our family teeth in private. Let us award the day a ranking of 10/10. Welcome to 2009 and all the good things it will bring. Peter continues to try and do battle with the lever arch file, so the element of stability remains.

Chapter Three - A new year and a new set of challenges

Saturday January 3rd 2009

Rising time 1.25 pm.

After an exciting and interesting morning, spent in completing several tasks and errands, I was faced with the horrible suspicion that Peter has taken a further tumble down into the abyss of Alzheimer's. I had been to buy him two new shirts, two new thermal vests and two new thermal underpants - long john variety - and was hoping that they would all fit comfortably. Breakfast seemed to go ahead in an orderly manner and Peter seemed quite coherent. He asked me if I was all right and appeared to wait for an answer. After having eaten his breakfast he made his way to the toilet. This was my cue for rushing in - very quietly - making the bed and lining up the clean clothes on the bed - in dressing order. It all seemed very quiet, so I went onto the landing to find the bathroom door firmly shut and the toilet door wide open. On opening the bathroom door I found Peter in a muddled and disorientated state. It was at this point that I realised that we were facing one of the more distressing elements of Alzheimer's cruelty. Loss of continence is something we all fear for ourselves, but the responsibility of managing a loved one's loss of continence is equally daunting. We cannot pretend that it is an easy situation to accept, but, in the absence of an alternative we have to get on with it. So now I will help Peter to put on his new clothes. They were all a perfect and generous fit. The day will have to rank as 6/10. Another slight change in routine will be that, now, he will have to be followed whenever he appears to be going to the toilet, in case he becomes muddled again. It will be a simple enough procedure, which can be done discreetly, so that Peter is not going to feel that he is being observed at all times. What a pity it has come to this.

Sunday January 11th 2009

Rising time 1.45 pm.

Peter appears to have settled on some particular plateau, which is resulting in some very amiable days. If this continues indefinitely we shall all be very happy and pleased with whatever is being achieved. I am going to take some credit for the situation and share it out, evenly, amongst all of us. Management is the key to some level of peace - not that we can always achieve peace - but it is so much easier to get it wrong. Consequently I feel we should note a mark in our favour whenever the opportunity arises. Even the wet clothing at the end of the day is not beyond management. It seems most probable to me that Peter's body is simply not responding quickly enough to the brain's message that he needs to wee. He is definitely receiving a message but, as he has to start trying to locate some place - any place - he is often too late. If I keep a constant eye on whatever he is doing, monitor every situation and lead him to the toilet, then there is a fair chance that he will make it in time. A poor aim is a hazard, but I am not quite sure what one can do about that - apart from being thankful for Mr Muscle's Floor Cleaner with Bleach and a few J.Cloths. The other slight problem is that he appears to be unaware of the fact that his clothes are wet, and any attempt to persuade him to change his clothes is met with resistance. But this must be because he has no idea why anyone should expect him to take off one set of clothing and put on another. It is not possible to put people into protective pads if they do not understand what they are for. Understanding is essential at some level. The only easy time would be if he happened to be unconscious - which would then present another range of issues. At present, if I can manage to keep one step ahead of him until the end of the day, the situation is more or less manageable. The washing is simple enough to manage, now that I have the equivalent of a nappy bucket carefully stored in the shower near the downstairs toilet.

Friday January 16th 2009

Rising time 4.15 pm.

Peter did get up, and have his breakfast at the normal time - namely around 1.30pm, but he must have been overcome by exhaustion because the effort of putting on his shoes proved to be too much to bear. He was forced to seek refuge in bed - fully dressed apart from shoes and smart jacket. He was very aggressive last night and did his best to shake me and try to push me over. Needless to say he did not succeed. Within a few seconds the rage had disappeared and he looked surprised and said, "Sorry." I have not worked out what caused the problem, except that it must have been connected with the undressing process, as all clothes were off apart from his vest and pants. I could have nipped smartly out of the way but it is important to know how long a frenzy can last and also how much strength can be raised. The amount of strength is not very great, so useful information has been learned with very minimal inconvenience. It would be difficult to accept if I thought I personally was responsible for the rage, but I am very certain that I am simply an obstacle which gets in the way sometimes. I can accept that, because there is nothing to be gained by fretting over something that does not exist. The day ranks as 6/10 - so far.

Thursday January 22nd 2009

Rising time 2.35 pm.

Although I had left Peter's breakfast within his reach he had not chosen to eat it. He was very comfortably settled in bed and in no obvious hurry to join the world. But, I have to say, that resting for hours in bed seems to be very beneficial as far as amiability is concerned. Bladder control is still a hit and miss affair - if you will pardon the pun. I shall continue to apply the agreed ranking criteria, but I shall not be sorry to reach the beginning of February, so that we can focus on a different skill. This monitoring system has, however, been of very great use because it keeps us close to the truth of the daily situation, rather than making a more or less educated guess about what may or may not have happened. Emergency furniture and floor protection systems, together with the monitoring of suspected toileting urges, are certainly helping me to feel slightly more in control of this stage than I was feeling at the beginning of the month. The other immensely useful piece of furniture, particularly from my viewpoint as Health and Safety Officer, is the white swivel chair we keep up in the bathroom. It makes undressing much easier, particularly where wet long-johns are concerned. Also for the removal of shoes. I am so glad not to have to struggle with double or even triple bows at the end of the day. Peter seems content to fasten his shoes himself with just one bow and, as far as I am aware, the shoes stay on the feet and he walks around in safety. One can hardly ask for more. I am hoping for a ranking of 7/10.

Monday January 26th 2009

Rising time 2.15 pm.

It is most fortunate that life has so many distractions. Should one be looking for companionship the search could end in very little. I rather think that I have been making a mistake when I have been working on the principle that Peter either likes, or needs, companionship now. When I have been making huge efforts to be in the Study, for two or three hours at a time during the evening, I have not been aware of a greater response than if I work elsewhere and pop into the Study from time to time and say, "Hallo." I am thinking now that, all the time he is warm, fed and comfortable, then he is not looking for anything else. He has his books and pieces of paper, he has plenty of scope for sorting and folding and is, I am now convinced, more than content with life in his solitary little world. Which does not mean that he should be left alone, but I do not think we have to feel quite so guilty about the other demands which take up our time.

Friday January 30th 2009

Rising time 2.05 pm.

Today has been a much better day all round. There is no earthly reason why I should be agitating about the time Peter is going to get up. If you look at Peter's life in a rational way then making the effort to get out of bed, to eat his breakfast, agreeing to help himself in the dressing process, wandering around while he tries to work out what he has to do - and then doing it - are activities which amount to work. It is the work he is called upon to do each day and, as he is not subject to a time inspection, he should be free to begin and complete his work in peace. I have been foolish enough to consider the getting up process as being a prelude to the day's, admittedly limited, activities, instead of seeing the process as being the beginning of the work. It is as important as any of the sorting and folding that goes on. But, I would prefer to regard the bath/bedtime process as a conclusion to the day's work. By that I mean I would prefer it to take the minimum amount of time - how selfish can one be? More selfish, I suggest, should the occasion arise! Yesterday I found most things very annoying but today has been much less so. Perhaps my own attitude is improving. Perhaps I have an attitude problem which is responding to an unknown force - coming from an unknown place. It is an interesting thought. Imagine drawing a pension and having an attitude problem. I am not certain whether to be glad or sad. I will hold on to the pension regardless of what happens about the A.P. I am fully expecting a ranking of at least 7/10. Hurray. Expectations realised - retrospectively.

Saturday January 31st 2009

Rising time 1.55 pm.

We have now reached the last day in January, and the final day for monitoring the degree of bladder incontinence which Peter is experiencing at present. It must be said though, that, as a result of the careful, if somewhat tedious monitoring, I have gauged the situation reasonably accurately and devised some sort of system for dealing with the problem. I was going to say dealing with the fall-out, but then I thought it an unfortunate choice of expression. Slightly funny, though. Life is manageable if I make absolutely sure that I am always one step ahead of Peter whenever he starts to wander out of the Study. I lead him towards the toilet, seat and lid raised at all times and point him in that direction. Sometimes he responds. That is the time to be on hand with the Mr. Muscle spray and the emergency rags. It is rather amusing to find that, after forty five years of *lowering* the toilet seat and lid, as a point of custom, I now find that not only am I now *raising* the seats and lids, but Peter is now, after forty five years of *ignoring* all seats and lids, making sure that, whatever else has been ignored or overlooked, seats and lids are now firmly *lowered*. Closed in fact. So, to finish this dull and uninspiring situation, I have to report that the coping and washing techniques seem to be paying dividends. I do hope I have managed to get this stage more or less under control. More would be better than less. A Ranking of 7/10 would be a wonderful end to the month - and could demonstrate some learning which, in itself, would be a matter of great relief.

Tuesday February 17th 2009

Rising time, 12 noon.

At the moment the lever arch is not co-operating very well but, with determination, Peter is doing his best to subdue it - or, more accurately, to knock it into some sort of shape.

You may have had an opportunity to hear, see or read the interview with John Suchet - a TV Reporter and Newsreader - who was talking about his job as carer for his wife, Bonnie, who was diagnosed with dementia several years ago. In the interview he mentioned that the very worst thing about Alzheimer's disease is that the sufferer has no idea that he or she has the disease. He found this a shocking and distressing fact. It is interesting to see how different people react to a given situation. I have always felt the best thing about Peter and Alzheimer's has been his ignorance of the fact that he had the disease. We had never moved beyond the furious acceptance of memory loss. The word Alzheimer's has never been mentioned by or between us. I am certain that had either of us considered it worthy of mention or discussion then we would have mentioned or discussed it. What, I wonder, is achieved, beyond panic and/or despair, if one has to face the prospect of having Alzheimer's disease as a diagnosis. I can see that if, in the future, early intervention with some effective medication offers a cure or, at least, a suppression of symptoms, then it may be a useful piece of information. If the sufferer is required to take some active steps in combating the disease then knowledge would be essential but I cannot, for the life of me, see that it would have done anything for Peter, except to concentrate his mind on ending his life. Memory loss was driving him to the brink. Knowledge could well have pushed him way beyond any sort of brink. In fact the sufferer's unawareness seems to me to be the only redeeming factor in the whole nasty business. As a carer I can regard the complaint as something that has removed the personality, and left a shell in need of care and attention. That shell cannot be held responsible for causing any hurt or upset, so things which would normally be regarded as totally unacceptable can, although still failing to be acceptable, be regarded as part and parcel of the caring package. On the other hand perhaps I have opted out of emotional connection with Alzheimer and all his works. Peter has now subdued the lever arch file and removed all the sheets from the file. At some point he will have to put them back. I will have to watch that space. With average luck he will not try to reassemble the file before it is time to get ready for bed. Then I can put the pages back in the file and leave it ready for further attention tomorrow. 9/10.

Wednesday February 25th 2009

Rising time 1.35 pm.

Another excellent day - thus far. Will it make 9/10. . ? Yes, it did. 9/10 it is!

Perhaps we should remind ourselves of the positive things about the way dementia has attacked Peter. By that I mean that some of the limitations, such as his inability to construct sentences, mean that we do not have to listen to the same one or two sentences being uttered throughout all waking hours. I would find that excessively difficult to manage and my patience would be sorely tested. Also, I can see that the practice of watching Peter when he is downstairs and making sure that, whenever he wanders around, he is encouraged to wander round to the downstairs toilet, has been fully justified. Provided this happens, the door is open and both seat and lid are kept raised, then the incidence of puddles is considerable reduced - probably by over half. It is a slightly tedious way of achieving one's objective, but it has the desired effect so it has to be worth doing. The lever arch file has been nudged into second place by the current favourite - a fully illustrated volume of *Britain from the Air*.

Sunday March 8th 2009

Rising time 1.55 pm.

Today has been a very good day for Peter in that he has been able to concentrate hard on his lever arch file, and on the pictures contained within the file. Most of the prints - of his own transparencies - have been arranged on the page so that they can be examined without turning the file round - i.e. they appear vertically on the page. A few pages have prints which appear horizontally. Now, until a few days ago, Peter had been content to turn the file in order to look at the horizontally arranged prints. But now he is distracted by them. He can see that the picture does not make sense when he looks at it. Or, at least, I think and hope that is what he sees and thinks. He has been struggling with the file in order to remove those pages. Having succeeded in removing two of the pages, he has spent some long time examining the prints and then trying to replace the pages in the file. But, as you will have already realised, the punched holes are in the wrong place! This means that the prints cannot be seen properly. Peter has tried every little trick he can think of to make the page fit in the file so that the horizontal prints appear as vertical prints - but, to no avail. Within the last few minutes he has come up with a solution. The answer is very simple. All one does is to fold the pages in half and slot them somewhere, anywhere, inside the file so that there is no overlap. The file is then closed and placed under the chair. When he gets up to straighten, line up, or fold the contents of the kitchen, I shall remove the folded pages, smooth them out and place them, out of sight, on top of the bookcase - along with two other pages which failed to please some time ago. This whole sequence of events does, undeniably, demonstrate definite brain activity. Another decision I have made is to stop using the term unco-operative. To be unco-operative pre-supposes some knowledge of being co-operative. If Peter has no idea of what is expected of him at any given time, then he is not in a position to be co-operative. By the same reasoning he cannot be unco-operative. Therefore, until further notice, the term *uncomprehending* will be used. We all know that the end result will be the same, but it seems unfair to accuse someone of behaving contrary to our wishes and expectations when that person is unaware of any such wish or expectation. Will this help with acceptance and tolerance? Who knows? Perhaps it will, if we can remember the new approach. The day ranks as 9/10 - mainly because all the Easter music has been prepared, sorted and filed ready for use at choir practice.

Friday March 13th 2009

Rising time 3.45 pm.

Breakfast was at 1.15 pm, but Peter found himself unable to make the necessary effort to leave his bed. When he was ready he was able to fasten the buttons on the cuffs of his shirt and has been quietly amiable throughout the remains of the day. It may be too early to fit the following observation into Peter's way of life, but I am working on the possibility that Peter is more settled in his activity if I am not physically present in the Study. Rachel has taken to working in the music room or upstairs and has sensed that Peter is no less settled as a result. If I am right in thinking that out of sight is out of mind, then there is also the possibility that, from time to time, the mind does not wish to be bothered with, or by, the sight. Again it may be that Peter has reached a new level in his creative activities, but there appears to be a significant reduction in the folding and sorting, and an increase in the studying and manipulating of the file. This could spell disaster in the orderliness of the kitchen. Last night I was forced to sort out several heaps myself. I shall watch this most carefully and see if I can attach any significance to what is happening. It is half past ten and I have been in the Study for half an hour, beaming, smiling and nodding. There has been one fleeting smile but no attempt to march anywhere or fold up any tea-towels. Spring may be in the air but it has not yet reached the step. Another valid point is, of course, that Peter is having what some might describe as the occasional off-day. One can only read the obvious body language as far as freedom from pain, discomfort and infection are concerned. It may be that Peter does occasionally feel that the effort of getting up is more than he can face. On the other hand he does not understand what is actually involved in getting up and so, perhaps, cannot prepare mentally for the event. I have given up worrying about the time he gets up. If it is after four o'clock, well, it is after four o'clock. I cannot force him out of bed, because he does not know what he is supposed to be doing. The end result is for him to clutch the duvet round him, close his eyes and cease to exist - until such time as there is some brain activity which prompts him to get up. The day ranks as 9/10.

Wednesday March 18th 2009

Rising time 7.00 am, with all the accompanying shock and horror occasioned by such an event.

Now there are several thoughts that have come into my mind. The first is undeniably selfish, because I found myself feeling decidedly irritated by the loss of my freedom this morning. Even though I had been able to complete the Wednesday morning commitments, I was still annoyed by the fact that I would not be returning to an all but empty house. I suspect that this caring role can develop and foster any underlying tendencies towards selfishness. As we all have large quantities of these tendencies it is probably inevitable. On the other hand it may well be that these tendencies act as a safety valve. They may keep the patient safe and so keep the carer out of the dock. This is partly, partly you note, a frivolous observation but the following thought is supposed to be slightly more appropriate to the circumstances in which we find ourselves. It relates back to the term *co-operation*. I will use Peter as an example of what must happen in many situations up and down the country. How on earth is one supposed to persuade Peter to get up out of his chair. I wanted him to stand up so that we could get on with the process of ending the day, getting the washing - of clothes and bodies - sorted out and to bring the day to an end. Peter was warm, comfortable, sleepy and happy. Why should he get up? He had no idea of the whys or the wherefores, and certainly no idea of the consequences. What happens in the beautifully-run Bupa Care Homes for persons with dementia? Are they forcibly removed from their chairs and frog-marched to the bathroom and then the bedroom, or are they given another blanket and left to slumber - possibly until the morning? I can see the potential for aggressive reactions here - possibly not only from the demented person! In conclusion I am more certain that the easier life is the one we live here in our house. My concern tonight will be to stay awake long enough get Peter upstairs, in the bath and into bed before he realises that he could take the easy way by falling asleep in the chair - playing silly tricks and pretending! I have every expectation of achieving bath and bed before one o'clock and shall expect to rank the day as 8/10 - in recognition of Peter's ability to stay awake throughout what has been an exceptionally long day.

Chapter Four - A matter of some light relief

Sunday March 22nd 2009

Rising time 1.35 pm.

It is as well that we ended the day when we did on Sunday, as the pantomime which became the end of Sunday evening was quite extraordinary. After what seemed to be a calm and peaceful evening, it seemed reasonable enough to try and end the day before one o'clock. All went well until the time came for Peter to take off his shirt. We had managed to negotiate the shoes, socks, tie, jersey and jacket. I had even managed to unbutton the shirt. It was then that the *no arms* trick took over. Peter suddenly decided that his arms no longer moved and sat determinedly and silently in the chair in the bathroom. My attempts to cajole, persuade, reason or even force the brain to respond and cause the arms to move, failed - emphatically, heroically and stubbornly. Then the face changed. I could see the faint stirrings of aggression and annoyance spreading into his face. I say *into* rather than *over* because *into* better describes the reality. He then said, most clearly, "Now What?" Now What, indeed. I suddenly felt far too tired to embark on one of these silly and intensely annoying episodes. So, I removed the discarded clothing from the bathroom and took myself out, closing the door behind me. I also advised Peter to remove his clothes and place them in the basket. Two instructions together, you ask. . ? The answer is *yes*, but, in total justification, I knew I was talking to myself. You will imagine my surprise when, on returning to the bathroom, I found that Peter had not only failed to remove any more of his clothes but had also managed to fasten, correctly, the seven shirt buttons and the two cuff buttons - buttons which are almost impossible to manage in daylight! In the end Peter wandered round the house, in the dark, because I had turned off all the lights. So I had a bath and got into Amber's bed and went to sleep within minutes.

Monday March 23rd 2009

Peter must have tired of wandering around because, by seven o'clock this morning, he was asleep in bed wearing his once-smart trousers, pants, vest and carefully buttoned shirt. The rest of today has been quiet. I am looking forward to a quiet night, if not a perfect end - quote from *Evensong*. What caused this hiatus? The only thing that was different was that I directed Peter into the upstairs toilet before taking him into the bathroom for a bath. I can only surmise that his brain was not expecting things to happen in this order. Peter was reluctant to come into the bathroom and seemed to be thinking of going downstairs. Some little loop was not working in my favour. Again can you see how easy it is for the management team to consider personal expectations, while imagining that it is the patient who is being considered. Or perhaps that is still the only way to cope. The day really does deserve 9/10.

Wednesday March 25th 2009

Rising time 1.45 pm.

Today has been a day of exemplary behaviour. Why? I do not know why, but I am very glad, as the Police Choir has a concert tonight. If we have worked things out in a careful and successful way, Rachel should arrive at her normal time and find Peter sitting, contentedly, in the Study. It has just occurred to me that the curtains will not be fully drawn when I leave - particularly as the very sunny point of today happens to be now - at five o'clock. Well, it will either prove or disprove a point - should such a point be relevant, or even exist. The Western Front is yours, Rachel.

"Curtains closed on my arrival at 7.30. Dad heading down the hall so I herded him to the toilet. Wrong destination at this moment but I paid the price later on. Again, Dad is not impressed with me, particularly if I am sitting on the floor instead of on the beanbag. I have moved upstairs and he seems to have forgotten about me again and has settled back to his photos. His face looks more fearful than I have seen for a long time. It reminds me of when he was still at the point when he knew you had gone out and would agitate from 9 pm each Wednesday. (Does this mean that his face expressed fear, or that he had a fearful face? Either way it must be avoided)."

I have to report a marked lack of success in preventing another accident this evening. There are some essential and practical implications to be considered in managing this stage of Alzheimer's disease. I realised at this moment that this new dimension to our family life was here to stay and, if we were to have any hope of coping sensibly with what was happening, then we would have to develop some coping strategies. Regretful acceptance, with perhaps an understandable touch of reluctance to accept the inevitable, will undoubtedly be the first emotion we shall have to confront. Having done this, we shall then get on with our responsibilities. Which leads me to another consideration.

I know I do not qualify for the Carer's Allowance - if you draw a full state pension you are automatically disqualified - but I am wondering whether I might suggest, and then apply for, a newly created Cleaner's Allowance. This would reduce the drain on the purse as far as Mr. Muscle's Floor Cleaner with added Bleach is concerned. What shall we rank? The day taken as a whole, or the day minus criminal offences. It could have been 9/10. On the other hand it may only be 2/10. Perhaps *Unclassified* is the better solution. In which case I shall take another jaunt on my bicycle.

It may be worth recalling that, thanks to Peter's exceptional memory for detail and his sound grasp of geography, he was, in January 1996, well able to help me with all the tiny details of our trip to Israel which I needed in order to write my, as yet, unpublished book, *Within Thy Gates*. How ironic that we can now benefit from his memory, while he remains 'lost in his head.' How cruel life can be. With this very much in mind I intend cycling over to the Mount of Olives, still in Jerusalem, and reminding myself of an extraordinary event in a rather beautiful spot. No sooner said than done. . .

I am in the Kidron Valley and looking towards the Mount of Olives. In 1995 Peter and I had completed a visit to see some of the original mud-brick walls of the ancient City of David, when we happened to glance over to one of the many olive groves which cover the Mount of Olives. There we saw a real family occasion being acted out. A fairly large group of men, women and children were all busily engaged in their own appointed tasks in the harvesting of the olives. The men seemed to have the nice easy job of sweeping up the stray olives while the women - wearing their white traditional clothing - ran up and down tall ladders, stretching out in what seemed to be a most precarious fashion as they endeavoured to pick the olives. They climbed ladders, they moved ladders and kept on working, very quickly, wherever they happened to be. The men kept pushing their brooms around plastic sheeting which covered the ground, while the small children alternated between rolling in the dust and emptying olives from small collecting baskets into the larger variety. While all this was going on, a camel, wearing its super red saddle, was standing behind the trees with its neck and head held high in the branches, quietly eating the profits. It was an absolutely hilarious and unforgettable sight. As a piece of stage management it could not have been bettered.

I shall cycle back with a smile on my face and joy in my heart.

Thursday March 26th 2009

Rising time 1.45 pm, preceded by a large puddle - in the upstairs toilet - which was discovered at 12.25 pm by the cleaning staff, who was not amused, as the mop is in danger of seeing too much in the way of active surface!

> *Applicants should attempt all of the following questions - bearing in mind there is no one correct answer, as that would be too simplistic - too unlike life!*

1. The first question to ask is this: How does one accurately define incontinence?

Constant and minute supervision has to be one requirement, for all waking hours, be those waking hours in bed, or up and about. What a tedious prospect.

2. What happens in the small un-noticed corners of the Bupa Care Homes, where floods and avalanches may not be noticed. Also who will volunteer to clean up, with the same high standard of meticulous hygiene we would expect in our own home?

3. Which parent would willingly and knowingly welcome the idea of their now young son or daughter, having, at some time in the future, to clear up after similar lapses from orderly behaviour - should that parent be in such a condition? Would you?

4. Husband or Wife? Well, it comes in as the *Worse* part in the *For Better, for Worse* clause, to which we subscribed.

5. Additional Question. Would I continue to do this if I were a partner? Probably? Possibly?

As an optimist, I am going to rank today as 8/10 at 8.50 pm.

Friday April 3rd 2009

Rising time 1.45 pm.

Peter has been very concerned today with the sheets of manuscript paper he has found on the kitchen table. I have been trying to write out some music, but have had to move upstairs in order to preserve my work, patience and sanity. I am more than a little concerned by the fact that Peter appears to have forgotten the purpose of a tea towel. He used to take a pride and pleasure in drying up the crockery and cutlery but, over the last few days, he has been content to stand with the cloth in his hand but has not been able to make any contact with the cups, etc. This has been a most useful skill over the last forty five years and I would feel sad to see another vital activity being eased out of use. He always seemed to enjoy drying-up, so it seems a poor substitute when he has to stand, look around, hold the cloth and yet ignore the work.

Sunday April 5th 2009

Rising time 2.25 pm.

Again it was very evident that Peter is much more able to cope with the shock of getting up and dressing when all possibility of being hurried has been removed. On balance there is rarely an overwhelming need for him to keep to my timetable rather than the one dictated by his own body. He has been much easier to manage at the end of the day and, provided there is no time pressure, he has not presented those dreaded refusals to be parted from his clothes. I still find it a very stressful and nerve-racking time of the day, but this is only because I am wanting the day to end so that I can get ready for bed. The bath looks so inviting that all I want to do is to jump in. Peter does still enjoy being in the bath, so that is a good reason for continuing the quaint old custom. The lever arch file has been set to one side, in order to make room for a *Student Atlas*. Peter is enjoying looking in this book and does try to work out some of the names of the countries. So, let us end on a note of triumph and award ourselves - and the day - a ranking of 10/10.

Easter Monday April 13th 2009

Rising time 1.55 pm.

This was a most reasonable hour at which to rise from one's bed. It might have been ten minutes earlier, but I opted to finish trimming the hedges and cutting the grass, as it is virtually impossible to do either of these jobs while Peter is in the garden. I was delighted with what had been achieved in the garden - which may have made me somewhat more amiable! But the whole day has been good. I ought to mention that the constant monitoring of toileting is proving to be helpful. The puddles have been reduced and I have decided that incontinence occurs when there is not only a failure to respond appropriately to the brain's directive, but also a lack of awareness of the existence of either a message or a directive. A very young baby is incontinent. An older person lacking awareness - due perhaps to disease, brain malfunction, paralysis or other physiological conditions - may well be incontinent but, for our purposes, I am going to suppose that, as Peter has been known to go searching for a quiet corner, then he must be aware of some connection between his brain and his bladder. This means that he is not incontinent. Rather his management skills are poor. Does that make any difference to us? Well, yes, I think it does make a difference, because I am still convinced of the value of leading him to the toilet whenever he gets out of the chair. This is how we all managed to potty-train our children, with the hope of them being able to manage the toilet by the time they started school. So, although it is highly unlikely that Peter will improve his understanding, he is, most definitely, able to respond to a level of suggestion. Fortunately there are other more satisfying and rewarding aspects in Peter's daily life and I am thankful that he does not have to be burdened with knowledge of his deteriorating condition. He does show definite signs of pleasure when engaging with his books and is sometimes happy to share them with me. Such moments make a significant difference to our ability to cope with the demands of life. The day deserves a ranking of 8/10.

Sunday April 26th 2009

Rising time 3.45 pm.

There was one notable feature about today. I returned from church at 12.50 pm, and went upstairs to see whether or not Peter had eaten the breakfast I had left, in readiness, on the chair next to the bed. I was somewhat surprised to see that he had eaten his cereal, but was more surprised to see that the jug of milk remained untouched. Then I realised what had happened. I had placed a glass of water on the tray, intending to place the glass of water on the chest of drawers, so that Peter had something to drink if he woke up feeling thirsty - and perhaps knowing that he was feeling thirsty. Foolishly I had failed to move it from the tray so, whenever Peter woke up, he must have gone to the toilet and then come back into the bedroom. He must have picked up the first container - a glass of water - and poured the contents over the cereal. I suspect that he knelt down on the floor to eat his breakfast, because the very full jug of milk was still very full. I do not think it remotely likely that he would have been able to carry the tray to the bed, sit down on the edge of the bed and then eat his breakfast, without spilling some of the milk from the jug. The black chair may well have looked like a table and so that might have set the scene for eating breakfast. I shall have to make sure I do not leave potentially confusing choices in Peter's path - or on his tray. Life is certainly much more congenial for Peter now he has an opportunity for a sleep after breakfast. But, he is now very, very, slow in completing the putting on of his trousers and the fastening of his belt. Shoes and socks also take an inordinate amount of time. Rightly or wrongly, I have decided that he does not need to spend long periods of time staring into space instead of dressing. If he is getting up later then it would seem reasonable for me to help with trousers, socks and shoes so that he can spend the time he is downstairs in a more productive way. I am wondering if Peter is spending less time in straightening and sorting and more time in staring at his pictures or, simply staring abstractly into space.

I think today deserves 10/10.

Tuesday April 28th 2009

Rising time 2.25 pm.

Peter is much more tottery on his feet and spends a great deal of his time downstairs resting and/or sleeping in the chair. Managing continence is still very much a challenge - and this will not change - but it is very important to keep looking for clues which might help in the management process. I have already detected a possible impediment. It will, I suspect, be necessary for me to remove the transparent protective runner I have placed, most carefully, on the floor by Peter's side of the bed. The problem results from Peter's overwhelming need to fold neatly and create as many right angles as possible. It is even possible that he is stopping to straighten the runner en route to the toilet. In which case there will be little hope of arriving at the toilet at the appropriate time. I would also say that Peter is calmer than I have ever known him to be in more than forty-five years. 9/10 would be a good ranking today, although perhaps I should take into consideration a determined assault on a lavender and chamomile spray air freshener. I have spent several years trying to remove the top of one of these sprays - for perfectly legitimate reasons which now elude me - but I have met with little or no success. Peter, without special training, has managed to achieve what the manufacturers - on health and safety grounds - may have hoped was impossible. Talent is a wonderful gift.

On a final note I must say that Peter appears to have no difficulty in kneeling down on the floor, to straighten up the occasional speck of fluff, or a book which appears to be out of alignment in the bookcase. He also spends some time in straightening the protective covers on his chair. When I consider how he totters around the house, it is astonishing to see how quickly he can pull himself into a half-standing position and then an almost upright position with minimal support. Today deserves a ranking of 9/10. The absence of comment on puddles means that they are now a normal part of the day and measures have been taken to minimise the inconvenience. These measures are sometimes very successful - and sometimes one wonders why one bothers!

Thursday April 30th 2009

Rising time 2.20 pm.

It is hard to grasp the fact that we have now completed one third of the new year we celebrated such a seemingly short time ago. When I look at the graph for this month I realise that, contrary to my own feeling, this has been a very good month with many peaks and a small handful of troughs. Three in fact. . . so take note! These last six hours have taken their toll on Peter's strength, so goodness knows what will have happened to his muscle tone. He is yawning steadfastly, so I may have to go and prepare the shower - and so run the risk of being able to get into bed before midnight. With that thought firmly in mind, I am going to award the day a ranking of 9/10 and go and heat up the shower room. This is a change of plan because I am planning to encourage Peter to have a shower instead of a bath. I suspect that, if I move the swivel chair into the shower room then he might find the washing process a little easier.

Tomorrow is May Day.

Stage Four

Chapter One - In which we search for signs of progress

Monday May 4th 2009

Rising time 2.25 pm.

If we are right in thinking that Peter had experienced another small bleed earlier on, in April, then I would say that he has recovered from any effects there might have been. This amiable and quiescent phase has the makings of a permanent condition - which would be to Peter's great benefit as well as everybody else's benefit. I have looked at today's situation and have found that it looks very much like yesterday's situation and also Saturday's. So, in anticipation of the consultant's planned visit a week on Thursday, I shall simply monitor this current state and see if I can find some reasonable question, or even hypothesis, to present to him. I think we would still like to know where Peter fits, on the UK Scale - which is very slim in comparison with the one operating in America - and whether or not there is any indication of what we might expect to see in the next stage. In fact, if we could actually pinpoint the whereabouts on the scale - and could access the scale - we could begin to think about any plans or adjustments we might need to consider. I am thinking in terms of any equipment, such as a suitable bed, should Peter's mobility deteriorate. It is rather fragile at the moment and we might have to join a queue of people hoping for what is carefully described as a *hospital bed.* I shall award the day 9/10.

Friday May 8th 2009

Rising time 2.45 pm.

It is extraordinary to see how fit, healthy and unlined Peter is looking these days. He seems to have shaken off the effects of a cold in a very brief space of time. Mine persisted for four weeks, but his had burnt itself out in three or four days. It is obvious that I shall have to try and be more cunning if I am to achieve a reasonable shower time tonight - although, I may be surprised and find that Peter is able to get on with the job without protesting. I know I have said that I was trying not to use the terms *co-operative* and *unco-operative*, as they were inappropriate if one has no understanding of the implications, but I wish we could have a little more of whatever replaces *co-operative* and a little less of what replaces *unco-operative*. Ranking will be 8/10. I am just noting that we have managed to leap over several hurdles tonight, with regard to the shower, and Peter is now in bed, having managed to wash his legs with a flannel. He is now exhausted and should be comfortably and quietly asleep in his bed . . . long before I have finished showering and bringing the day to an end .

Saturday May 9th 2009

Rising time - we are still waiting and it is now eleven o'clock in the evening.

Peter may have made a deliberate decision not to get up today. On the other hand he may simply have failed to notice the passage of time and the arrival and departure of the hours of daylight. For whatever reason he has spent the day in bed. He has had his breakfast and dinner sitting on the edge of the bed; he has managed several trips to the toilet -

unaided; at seven o'clock this evening he put on his clean blue shirt, over his pyjama jacket and then got straight back into bed. He has managed to resist my attempts to get him into his clothes, but he has been perfectly happy with his current status quo. Austin has given me a lovely bottle of wine so I have decided to round off an excellent and productive day - I have managed to sort and clear the garage and take the rubbish to the tip - which was a wonderful example of respite, believe it or not. The day ranks as a very generous 12/10. Criticisms and adverse comments directed at the care staff will go unheeded, as she has gone off duty. Before I raise my glass I must note an article, from America, in which it seems to have been proved, beyond all reasonable doubt, that anyone caring for an elderly or vulnerable person will prolong their life expectancy. This could be a subject for serious discussion, or at least quiet contemplation. At the moment I am not quite sure as to *whose* life expectancy could be prolonged. The word *their* is somewhat ambiguous. The very thought has made me feel very excited, elated, confident and very anxious to drink my glass of fine red wine - which will, of course, benefit *my health* on Sundays, Tuesdays, Thursdays and Saturdays, while doing me *great harm* on Mondays, Wednesdays, Fridays and the following Sunday! Twas ever thus.

Friday May 15th 2009

Rising time 2.40 pm.

Peter has been amiable and busy with his straightening operations. I think it would be fair to say the volume of straightening achieved in any given time does seem to be rather less than in previous months. However, he is still finding time to attend to his muscle tone, as he is very keen on keeping the hall door mat straight. This demands plenty of kneeling down, stretching out of arms and then standing upright again. This may sound flippant but, if we put it in the context of yesterday's meeting with the consultant, it may turn out to be an important contribution in the maintenance of Peter's well-being. After reading a brief synopsis of the last six months doctor observed that there seemed to be some small change in the condition. He also decided, after trying to hold some sort of conversation with Peter, that there had been some further cognitive deterioration. It was interesting and reassuring to hear that, although Peter's actual condition was now in the severe stage, his overall appearance and level of calm was presenting a less severe slip. To put it in its simplest terms, he considered that Peter presented rather better than he was. I was interested to hear how, with this condition, someone could be more ill than he appeared to be. Doctor thought that it was because he was in an environment with a very tight structure, a minimum of disruption and a routine that catered for his needs. It all sounded simple and straightforward. The quality of common sense also appeared to be helpful. I did point out that every single member of the family had his or her own specific contribution which was essential to overall care. It was interesting to hear something about the most frequent reason for people having to be relieved of the burden of care. We will all have our own understanding of how different problems cause different reactions between people trying to hold together a situation which becomes more and more demanding. We need to maintain the environment! Today ranks as a 9/10 day.

Thursday May 21st 2009

Rising time 2.00 pm.

I forgot to mention that, on Wednesday afternoon, Peter found a large jar of *Carte Noir* coffee and poured a small quantity of water into the almost full jar. Obviously I was not able to tolerate such waste, so I added sufficient boiling water to the contents of the jar and, scoop by scoop, managed to transfer the now liquid contents to a one litre size empty milk flagon. If you recall the rather elderly advertisement for *Camp Coffee* you will immediately recognise the nature of the brown liquid I am now pouring into the coffee cups. Fortunately the flavour remains unchanged and I can see no reason for that situation to alter - all the time the Liquid Coffee is kept in the fridge. I am sorry if my reaction seems somewhat extreme, but I really could not allow such gross waste of an excellent coffee. So what did I learn? Quite simply, continue to hide all food and drink which might attract attention. 7/10.

Sunday May 24th 2009

Rising time 2.50 pm.

Today has been a very good day during which a great deal has been achieved. Consequently I shall award the day 9/10 and try and bring the very good day to an end. On second thoughts, and at ten minutes past midnight, I have to note that, for some as yet unknown reason, Peter decided that he would only allow one shoe - the left one - to be removed and no other clothing. Not even the right shoe. It may be very weak and feeble of me, but I have decided that I am not going to continue the struggle tonight. Weakly and feebly I am going to have a bath and go to bed. Peter is now sitting in the Study considering the new *English Heritage Magazine*. The ranking could descend to zero but that would be unfair as the rest of the day has been worth 9/10. I shall close down the computer and run a bath.

Monday May 25th 2009

Rising time - this is scarcely relevant, as Peter did not actually manage to lie down.

Having said that, I was profoundly shaken to find Peter wandering around the house just before eight o'clock this morning. I have not quite abandoned my question over the possibility of the brain needing to recharge its batteries, but it may be necessary to adjust the thinking. I could be tempted to think that sitting up in a chair for seven and a half hours has been most beneficial to Peter. Although he shows no sign whatsoever of being tired, I shall continue to look carefully for any sign of fatigue and then try the shower routine. One interesting thing happened this afternoon. I was taking the opportunity to sort through the pictures when, to my great astonishment I found a print of the interior of a Church which I realised I knew intimately. It was none other than St. John's. It was in Peter's collection and instantly recognisable - after the five years we spent in and around it. Not only did I find the interior but I also found a photograph of Peter conducting a Wedding Service in St. John's Church. Towards the end of the afternoon, when Peter had finished sorting out the tea spoons, I took him over to the piano and showed him the exterior of St. John's. He stared at it, pointed at it and then said, "Ah...Yes!" I then showed him the picture of the interior. He stared at it intently for some little while and then made the sign of the cross. I had the strange feeling that, on looking at the picture he had, in his brain, gone into the Church and down the aisle. I felt that he was connecting with something in his brain. Did he know that this was the first church where he was the Priest rather than the Curate? Did he, in his mind, enter the Church and feel moved to make the sign of the cross - which would have been entirely normal, of course. When I consider the large number of pictures of church interiors he examines each day, I have to say that I have never seen him cross himself when looking at them. What a wonderful thing it would be if he could still recall, however distantly, that he served as a priest in that church.

I shall award the day a ranking of 9/10.

Sunday May 31st 2009

Rising time 2.35 pm.

As this is the last day of the month it would be appropriate to make some sort of comment on what appears to have been happening with Peter - although conjectures are becoming rather more repetitive.

It seems a rather pathetic point to make but I shall make it, nevertheless. If we accept that stress is an essential and entirely normal part of the human condition then, perhaps, it is reasonable to suppose that reactions to those levels of stress are also essential and normal - however unwelcome they may be. It has not taken much thought to work out that, for me, the most stressful component of the day is waiting to see if Peter is going to find himself able to get up from his chair at the end of the day and allow himself to have a shower and a hair wash. It is necessary to shower and hair wash every time he co-operates, although I would remind you that it is a word I am not using willingly. The truth is that any alternative sounds more than a little contrived. But, there is a need to take advantage of every opportunity, so that the night he stays unwashed and sleeping in his chair in the Study does not become totally unacceptable. I can never be sure whether or not he is going to get up and put on his day clothes, so it does seem rather silly for me to decide to worry about whether or not I am going to be able to get them off again. Perhaps I should worry about getting them on? Perhaps I should worry about something else? Or, perhaps I should stop worrying altogether and get on with the job I am supposed to be doing. But I am doing that anyway, so perhaps I shall stop this new found skill called Twitter - computer talk not bird talk - and get ready for bed. The day will be another 10/10 and May can leave on a high.

Monday June 1st 2009

Rising time 1.55 pm.

I am very glad May went out on a high because I am entertaining some slight doubts about the beginning of June. It would be tedious in the extreme to have to spend the whole of the month discussing inappropriate urination, but, the signs are there. A ranking of 7/10 would be encouraging!

Saturday June 6th 2009

Rising time 2.15 pm.

I have, reluctantly, to express some concern over Peter's muscle tone. His walking skills have deteriorated significantly and his shuffling gait is now accompanied by a marked lopsidedness. He is also experiencing some problems with his balance. But, I must add that, each evening - or any evening when he is going to agree to the shower/bed routine - I do try and engage him in a tug of war game whereby I try to pull him out of the chair. I can manage the tug of war whereas I cannot manage to haul him out of the chair - because of my silly arms, not Peter's weight, which seems stable at nine stones four pounds. My thinking behind the tug of war is, firstly, that it is a somewhat absurd thing to do and Peter is sufficiently distracted by its absurdity to forget to object to getting out of the chair. The next important point is that I have some idea as to how long it takes him to establish his equilibrium before starting to walk. I can also see how much transference of weight is needed before he is able to walk across the room. I do not, so far, count tottering as walking. Today he has been very sleepy and has not been able to work out how to clean his teeth or even shave. He was, however, very delighted with the result when I used a safety razor. I am not very good with the Braun razor so I do hope this is just a passing blip.

But today has been a day devoted to stalking, moving items and vocalising. I am none the wiser, but I do know that I find this constant scrutiny of whatever I am doing more than a little annoying. It is a good job the mouth knows how to maintain a smile. Nature knew a trick worth two! One point has struck me in the past few minutes. I was looking over the graph for May and I realise that it looks very bright and cheery. Not everything was really all that bright and breezy, but I am wondering if, as the skills fail and the frailty becomes more evident, perhaps we make more allowances. This could result in behaviour, which would once have merited a ranking of perhaps 5/10, finding itself accepted as 7/10. As the disease progresses we cannot keep marking down as there is every possibility that every achievement has made greater demands on the patient. I shall have to reflect on this idea. In recognition of this I shall award a ranking of 8/10 - even though it seems a most generous ranking - under the circumstances!

Monday June 8th 2009.

Rising time 2.05 pm.

The term 'rising time,' in today's context, has much more to do with a series of most unfortunate events, which even Lemony Snickett would have difficulty in creating. Yesterday's ranking was far from appropriate. It could have moved into the negative market but that would have been like awarding a child a good grade for a piece of classwork and then reducing the grade because he or she could not manage to behave properly in the playground. So it can stand as it is, but . . . So what exactly happened? After a relatively quiet evening, Peter suddenly, at around ten o'clock, decided to tidy up the kitchen. The kitchen has always to be tidy, in order that Peter can find enough room to organise his tidying programme. When I went into the kitchen Peter was sitting at the table, sorting out a cloth bag containing some of Joe's brightly coloured marbles. He was deeply engrossed and seemed very happy. At midnight I decided to try and set the shower/bedtime routine in operation. There was some initial reluctance to come into the shower area - which I put down to Peter not understanding what was required. However he eventually came in and sat down on the swivel chair. Shoes, socks, jacket and jersey were all removed without fuss or contradiction. I even managed to unbutton his shirt. This proved to be the end of whatever passed for co-operation. I had turned on the shower to remind Peter that the water was there waiting for him. He nodded at it and then, without further ado, stood up and started to fasten the buttons of his shirt. I pointed to the running water and suggested that we undo the buttons again when That Look came over his face. He then said, in a most aggressive fashion, "What are you?" As I have yet to work out the answer to that question, I refrained from making any comment. Peter then flapped his arms, assumed a boxing stance and then seized me by the arms and tried to shake me vigorously. The strength and vigour was very evident in the face, but very lacking in the arms. He then stopped and slapped my face - once with each hand. Again the strength was in the face and lacking in the hands - which was just as well as I might have been tempted to attack him - with considerable strength and vigour. I left him, with his clothes, in the utility room, turned off the lights and went up to run a lovely lavender and chamomile bath. I then went to bed - in our bedroom. The time was almost one o'clock. At a quarter to three I heard Peter moving about downstairs. He came upstairs - which surprised me - came into the bedroom, looked out of the window, opened the chest of drawers and then went out, taking care to try and close the door. He then went downstairs. At half past four he came up again and went into the toilet. I put on the bedside light, turned back Peter's side of the bed and then went quickly into the children's room and put the bean bag against the door before getting into Amber's bed. All seemed very quiet. When I got up at seven o'clock and looked into the bedroom I found Peter fast asleep in bed. After collecting Joe and completing the morning's work, I took Peter's breakfast up and noted, with considerable surprise, that his shirt, jersey, trousers, socks and jacket were all reasonably arranged on the chair. This meant that Peter would be wearing his vest and pants in bed. I felt certain that I would not only be washing his underclothes but also the bedding, but, to my immense relief and astonishment, when he got out of bed I could see that his vest and pants were dry and clean. So far so good. After breakfast I decided that dressing for the day should start immediately. Peter did not protest and so that job was quickly and reasonably accomplished. He has been quiet and passive today, although there has been rather too much of the limpet syndrome. I have been more concerned about my own reaction. It may sound very petty but I have felt more than a little outraged by his behaviour last night. Even though I am fully aware that he has no recollection of what he did, I still found myself not wishing to be in the same room with him. How stupid is that? I shall expect to have recovered my equilibrium tomorrow, but I have also worked out another plan of action, which should prevent either of us being placed in that situation again. The minute Peter refuses to comply with the undressing stage before showering I shall abandon the idea, and leave him to organise himself in any way he chooses and I shall go to bed. I shall also leave the bed arranged in such a way that, should he come upstairs, then he might be reminded that he can get into bed - with or without his clothes - and go to sleep. In the meantime I shall be sleeping in the other room. So, with that cunning plan in mind, I shall compromise the ranking as 5/10.

Chapter Two - Another flight from responsibility

Saturday June 20th 2009

Rising time 2.15 pm.

Today is the Twelfth Anniversary of Peter's ordination to the Roman Catholic priesthood. He has spent his celebration day very quietly indeed. I have tried to leave everything in good order for the next thirty-six hours as Joe and I are going to drive down to Farnham at six o'clock tomorrow - Sunday morning - and will be returning at six o'clock on Monday evening. It is a short trip but we have been looking forward, for the last three weeks, to what has become our annual pilgrimage to the South. Rachel is making this possible so I hope everything will go smoothly for her. Thank you so much, Rachel. I hope your promotion to the rank of Senior Care Co-ordinator and General Purpose Carer brings you much satisfaction and not too much extra work. Say *NO* to challenging behaviour and please do not spend too long looking for the wine, as I could not find any when I was looking for some. It must have been enjoyed by person or persons unknown. The day deserves at least 11/10.

Care Plan for the period Sunday June 21st and Monday 22nd June 2009

By including this Care Plan I hope to give the reader a slightly clearer idea of the level of deterioration in Peter's health and general condition over the last twelve months. Each detail of the Care Plan has had to be carefully considered, in order that Peter's care is as supportive as possible. There is an equal degree of importance attached to the need for the carer to be in a position to follow the plan, and so have as stress-free an experience as possible. I am so grateful to Rachel for her willingness to assume these responsibilities, and still to keep smiling.

In order to achieve the smoothest regime possible it is strongly recommended that the Carer adheres to the plan and resists the temptation to implement untried methods or routines. Be creative, by all means, but only within the framework of the schedule. The author disclaims responsibility for most things in life and this Care Plan is no exception!

Sunday June 21st 2009

Check the toilets.

1. Whenever you choose to arrive you will find the breakfast tray resting on the black chair in the bedroom. The breakfast may be in the dish, or it may have been eaten. If it has been eaten, remove the tray from the bedroom and take it downstairs, so that it does not become another distraction or cause for a one-sided conversation.

If the breakfast has not been eaten, draw the curtains. Pour the milk from the jug onto the cereal and then stand by the bed, smiling and suggesting that Peter might like to eat his breakfast. The time, ideally, should be no later than half past one - in the afternoon. He should then sit up, unaided, with his legs reaching to the floor, which will allow you to place the tray, steadily, on his lap. He will need the medication before he has eaten too much breakfast. Once he has started to eat you are free to leave him until he has finished - usually within ten minutes.

2. You will find the medication, clearly labelled, in the second of the four kitchen cupboards - top shelf. Place on a teaspoon and offer to Peter, with some water, which you will have put in a glass.

3. When you are ready, make and take up a cup of tepid coffee and stand by the bed, smiling and suggesting that he might like a drink. He should then sit up and take the cup. At this point ease the duvet towards the end of the bed, but do not be tempted to fling it on the floor. This will arouse his suspicions and he will suspect that he might have to get up - which, of course, will not be part of his plan. When he has had enough to drink, take the cup and place it on the chest of drawers, where it will not be a problem. Now for the next stage.

4. You will see the clothes, arranged in order, resting on the chest of drawers.

Still smiling, and talking pleasantly about the day being lovely - regardless of the truth - you should hold the vest, in the appropriate fashion, in order to get it over his head but do not attempt to try and take off the pyjama jacket before the vest is resting on the shoulders. If possible undo the jacket buttons and slide the garment in the traditional way, taking care not to touch the skin - especially if you have chilly fingers. Once the vest is on, seize the shirt - and the opportunity - and thread the arms through the sleeves. Fasten the buttons. He may try to fasten the cuff buttons. He may succeed. If not, you do it, but fasten the first button so that the cuff is as large as possible. No interference with muscle tone will be required here.

I would leave the tie near him, in case he wants to have a go with it. I would not suggest that you try yourself as it has to be at exactly the right length and we could, as a result, be having to consider overtime payments.

Regardless of the weather put on the jersey. Remember, he may have to sleep in the chair and so will need to be warm enough.

Now for the pyjama trousers. If he co-operates, by levering himself up on the side of the bed, you may be able to pull them down to his knees before he falls back on the bed. Feed the legs into the underpants and, before pulling up the pants, ease the socks onto the feet. Do not pull too roughly. I would suggest that you then tell him to pull up his pants, tuck in his vest - but not his shirt - and then, when he is sitting down repeat the operation with the trousers. (This time he will need to tuck the shirt into the trousers). If you have got this far then you have done very well and you should then put on the shoes and tie the laces before letting him pull up the trousers. You can try and make the bed, or else leave it until later. You may feel like going for a power nap but there is not really sufficient time. You can leave him to finish his dressing. You will, of course, be fully accepting of how he appears at the end of the exercise. No photo shot has been planned, so do not be too critical of the level of sartorial elegance.

5. It could now be time to come downstairs. Load the toothbrush - if in doubt refer to last year's Care Plan - and press the tap so that Dad can see the water rushing out, at considerable expense, as this will remind him as to what he is supposed to be doing. If, by this time, you have managed to get Dad dressed for the day you should be downstairs and possibly in the kitchen.

6. Assuming that the teeth have been cleaned it would now be an idea to sort out the chin. I suggest that you offer Dad the razor and, if necessary, direct it towards his face. He does often try to clean his teeth with the razor, but it is not as effective as a conventional toothbrush. Consequently it should be discouraged - or, if that is too negative an approach, you might refrain from encouraging.

7. The next item on the agenda is the eating of the apple, which you will see in the dish by the kettle. Should you suspect that breakfast was eaten early, then additional calories, in the form of one or two plain digestive biscuits, can be offered with the apple. The apple is more likely to be eaten if offered whole. I have found that quartered or sectioned apple pieces tend to be hidden in odd places or even left uneaten in the bowl.

8. Dinner time is any time between half past five and half past six - depending on the rising time, should you have been so lucky as to have had a rising time.

A very generous serving of pasta, mixed vegetables, home-made quorn chicken supreme and two spoons of baked beans should fill the plate, which can then be heated in the microwave. Use the benefit of a university education to calculate the required time. You could, in complete safety and without any form of compromise, even use the mouth test to see when it is ready. Your mouth, preferably. When ready, and if you are being stalked or supervised, place the hot plate of hot food on the tray, with the spoon and fork, and carry it into the Study. Dad may or may not sit down without encouragement.

The appropriate medication - the pot with the blue spot - should be given, in the Study, with Peter sitting down. Watch him swallow the tablets and discourage him from removing them from his mouth in order to look at them. You know all this, Rachel, and do not need me to tell you but, just in case someone else has to do this job instead of you, it is necessary for the tips to be recorded.

When ready, the Harrington's Square, on the radiator in the kitchen, should be tucked into the V of the V-necked jersey and arranged over the lap. The tray is then placed on the lap and Dad should be able to enjoy his dinner, using the fork in his left hand, while you make sure that any washing-up has been done. This is essential because any washing-up water is a signal for washing the hands, soaking the arms of the suit and splashing, vigorously, the rest of the already-mentioned suit. It sounds silly but, by this stage in the day, it is better to reduce, as far as possible, the opportunities for unintended annoyance or irritation.

The lovely pot of yoghurt should only appear after the dinner plate has been removed. If spotted earlier it can be mistaken for a savoury sauce and poured over the dinner. The dinner would be eaten, but the taste buds might be a little confused.

9. Tepid coffee can be offered after the meal has been eaten. Offering the coffee simply means placing it on the dinner-mat resting on the small table by the chair in the Study. It may or may not be drunk during the course of the evening.

10. Once you have dealt with the washing up - which

includes drying up and putting the equipment wherever is convenient for you - you could allow yourself to enjoy a well-deserved sense of achievement. Of course it may all be re-ordered during the course of the evening, but that is only to prevent you from feeling in control of the situation - any situation.

11. At around ten o'clock you can give the medication from the pot with the red spot – with water and a replacement cup of coffee, if appropriate.

You will be the best judge as to whether or not it is necessary for you to be sitting in the Study. Some companionship is required but sometimes constant companionship can make Dad restless. Remember to make good your escape whenever you need to.

After some considered and careful thinking I would suggest that you do not attempt to get Dad ready for bed.

If you decide to leave him in the Study to sleep then the following conditions would be helpful.

LEAVE ON THE FOLLOWING LIGHTS THROUGHOUT THE NIGHT: Kitchen light over the sink; light in the downstairs toilet; hall light; upstairs toilet light; small lamp on my side of the bed.

Remove the velvet cover and fold back the duvet - lengthwise - so that Dad can get into bed and cover himself up if he wishes.

You are then free to go to bed when you are ready. Normal washing facilities are readily available, but the bath will take a little while to fill up, on account of the lower water pressure. Please remember to place the bean bag against the door of your room before you get into bed. Sleep well.

Monday June 22nd

If Dad is in bed, place his breakfast tray on the chair before you leave the house. Also please place a glass of water - half-filled - on the mat on the chest of drawers. Leave the medication in the kitchen cupboard until you are ready to give it to him yourself.

I cannot imagine that there will be a dressing routine to follow - unless the clothes are wet. A clean set, consisting of jacket, trousers, vest, pants, shirt, tie, socks and shoes can be found on the computer table next to the main computer. Clean pyjamas are in the second drawer of the chest of drawers. I will have to leave this unknown situation for your own resolution. . .

Whatever happens, at some point to suit you, the teeth cleaning and shaving routine can be followed.

If, by chance, Joe and I have not arrived home by six o'clock perhaps you will repeat the dinner ritual for me.

I do hope you can find something to eat, something to interest you and anything else you might need.

Remember, you do not have to be here all the time - provided the inside door is securely locked as well as the back door.

As far as extra calories are concerned - for the Carer and the Cared For - I am delighted to leave that to your discretion.

Rachel's comments:

> **"Some thoughts on where we are up to.**
>
> "Dad lives in the shadow lands now. There is no sense of caring for a person you know. The face is no longer familiar.
>
> "Dad has no receptive language and extraordinarily little understanding of non-verbal communication, other than facial expression - which he is obviously depending on for almost all his information.
>
> "He frequently recognises objects only when they are functioning, not by their appearance or place.
>
> "Our presence troubles his stillness, but the stillness also troubles him. The balance is difficult to judge.
>
> "There is no joy. Pleasure is so fleeting - and is probably more about seeking a level of reassurance than actual pleasure.
>
> "He is clearly safe here, and the uncertainty and constant wandering is because you are not here, Mother. There is an indication of how appalling it would be for Dad to have to make any move - initially at least."

Thank you **so** much, Rachel. You are so much more than the proverbial star. It seemed such a lovely long time while we were away. You have proved yourself a first class Care Co-ordinator - and a very difficult act to follow. If I fail to make the grade I shall know where to come! So please remember those famous words, "Your country needs you!"

Tuesday June 23rd 2009

Rising time - before 12.55 pm.

Peter was more than ready to get up, and has spent a long time moving about in a way that suggests that he is checking out the territory. He then went into the Study for another sleep. He was still asleep at four o'clock when I arrived back with Molly and William. Amber and Joe arrived home from school at about the same time, so everyone was able to enjoy a very happy hour or so before it was time to return children to parents. At the moment I feel that Peter has settled back into whatever was his normal routine. He seems to accept that I am here on my own and has stopped looking for people to pop up from nowhere. He is holding a very long and complicated talk on the *National Trust Book for 2006*, although I suspect that he is actually discussing the large hole he has managed to make in the first few pages. It would be dishonest for me to pretend that I have returned from my holiday with a higher tolerance level of inane twitter, but at least I can run off to Surrey, in my mind, while attempting to make encouraging responses to the thoughts on the National Trust. It will soon be bedtime so I shall rank the day as 9/10 - and be thankful for Rachel's kindness in allowing me some escape.

Thursday June 25th 2009

Rising time 1.35 pm.

Today has seen a great improvement in Peter's general level of peace and contentment. He has allowed himself to sleep and sit quietly, without agitating about anything in the home. I feel that whatever he was experiencing, during my thirty-six hours in Surrey, has been put in a secure place somewhere, and the uncertainty he was feeling has been replaced by peace and calm. So I shall close the day with a ranking of 8/10 and hope for a quiet night.

Thursday July 2nd 2009

Rising time 3.30 pm, following a shocking pantomime on Wednesday evening. It is possible, in fact probable, that the presence of another person, namely Cousin John, is proving rather difficult for Peter either to accept or ignore.

Last night's shower time was a signal for Peter to start upon a course of disruptive, defiant and confusing behaviour. There was the display of aggression when he was supposed to be taking off his trousers before getting in the shower. This meant that, wearing only underpants and trousers, he was ready to spend the night interfering with light switches, doors, movable items on shelves and even curtains. At three thirty he did his best to open John's bedroom door but failed, due to the strategically placed beanbag. At half past four, my patience having disappeared, just as the sun appeared, reminding me that the hours of resting were dwindling rapidly and I was unlikely to manage much more than a few more minutes actual sleep, I retrieved him from the bathroom and instructed him, quietly and firmly, to get straight into bed. Whereupon he smiled and sat on the edge of the bed, pretending that his legs and feet were attached to the floor and could not be eased into bed. I found this difficult to believe, so I seized both feet and found, to Peter's surprise, that they were more than capable of being placed on the bed and then being covered with the duvet. Yes, I know we are in the middle of a heat wave but, if Peter is not under a duvet, he has no means of knowing that he has to stay in bed. When I came downstairs at half past seven in the morning he was sitting comfortably in his chair in the Study! He was fast asleep and clutching the *National Trust Handbook* for 2009. After he had eaten his breakfast I took him back to bed. Three o'clock came and he was able to get up and get dressed. The day followed its accustomed pattern. John has enjoyed a day of relaxation but I do think he is finding Peter's physical presence - even in the adjoining room - somewhat disconcerting. An amendment for yesterday is more than justified but the graph will have difficulty coping with my recommendation. Perhaps all ranking should really be retrospective, but I feel this could lead to negativity of thought as well as the potential for a negative ranking.

Monday July 13th 2009

Rising time 1.05 pm.

To my immense astonishment - and great delight - Peter rediscovered a long lost skill. We had just started the dressing process when I had to go and answer the phone. I left Peter sitting on the bed surrounded by the clean clothes he would be putting on. On my return he had taken off the pyjama jacket, put on the vest - the right way round - and was staring at the floor. There was no problem in putting on the rest of the clothing and he even adjusted his right sock to make it more comfortable. 9/10

Friday July 17th 2009

Rising time 1.45 pm.

Do not fall into the trap of thinking that you can appear to be concentrating on another person, with impunity, while you are full of your own ideas, activities, plans, etc. While doing exactly that and encouraging Peter in folding up his blue handkerchief, I have just discovered that I was actually encouraging him to tear holes in the handkerchief. It was an elderly piece of cloth which had reached that stage whereby its softness would have been greatly appreciated by a sore nose. Peter has been holding it up and, as I now realise, pulling on the holes in two of the corners while I am nodding in agreement and making encouraging noises. He needed no encouragement. The man who can massacre fly spray and a lever arch file has proved himself to be equally competent in the field of shredding. Life may appear to be sedentary here at home but, at the moment, some definite toning and endurance is taking place. The pieces of blue handkerchief are being neatly and carefully arranged on the table by the window. I think I may have forgotten to mention that survival is almost guaranteed if whatever - and I mean whatever - goes on in the home is regarded as normal. The bookcase is posing something of a problem now, as some books seem to have been arranged on their sides. I think I shall stay and keep watch in case they are forced into very small places. The reason some are on their sides is very simple. They are too tall to stand upright. One of the culprits is a book on Yvres Congar, a renowned and learned Christian thinker. It may prove to be bedtime reading. That looks unlikely now, as Peter has just managed to hide it behind a thick reference book on French grammar. We can breathe again and award the day 9/10.

Sunday July 19th 2009

Rising time - has yet to happen.

Last night's shower time descended into another pantomime of no-comprehension and therefore no going along with the undressing routine, once it was time to take off the trousers. Fortunately, in a way, it was a cold evening so I was obliged to leave Peter wandering around a chilly house in bare feet and wearing only his trousers and underpants. I prepared, noisily, for a shower until, eventually, the chill factor had some effect and Peter came into the utility room - looking for some sort of warmth? This time he was glad to take off his clothes and stand under the warm water. Actually getting into bed appeared to be difficult but it was managed. It is now almost three o'clock on Sunday afternoon and he has refused two offers of coffee - although he has eaten his breakfast. I have yet to decide whether this is a further indication of another tiny downward descent or whether he just does not wish to get up - which feeling we will have to ignore if the world is to continue rotating on its axis

It was just after half past five when Peter eventually discovered that he did really want to get up and dress. So, having achieved that small miracle, the timing fell into place. I am going to award the day 9/10.

Thursday July 24th 2009

Rising time 2.45 pm.

Peter was up and wandering around at half past nine, so, having changed his pyjamas, I gave him his breakfast. He does not seem to realise what is amiss and seems really astonished when I attempt to change the clothes, but - and I do not think I am mistaken - he does register that life is more comfortable in dry clothes. It rather looks as though the problem is not registered, or, if it is registered, then it is certainly not understood. So there is no understanding that a solution might be to hand. But the solution is acknowledged by an approving expression on the face. I applaud the advice I am offered, which is to try and let Peter get used to protective pads, but no one has yet explained to me how I fix them to the body, when there is no understanding of their purpose. I am prepared to accept the excellence of the plot - forewarned is forearmed - but I am failing in the logistics department. So, until I become more competent I shall have to continue mopping up and washing more and more clothes. The day itself has been very good so a ranking of 8/10 is indicated.

Friday July 25th 2009

Rising time 1.35 pm.

The day has been very good indeed. I have got on with my writing and Peter has been happy resting in the chair. Another factor to consider is whether or not a riser chair might be a good idea. With this in mind I have left a message with the occupational therapist, to ask for advice. I have also bought a stair gate from Mothercare. Of course the existence of the banister rail and the other grab rail does affect the type of gate which can be used -and also it has to be removed each morning. I have set up a Heath Robinson affair at present which could prove to be effective, but, only time will tell. Tomorrow morning to be precise. The aim of the gate is, obviously, to discourage Peter from going downstairs. Perhaps it should be fitted with bells in order that I can be summoned! The day deserves 9/10 - and fingers crossed for a quiet night.

Wednesday July 30th 2009

Rising time 2.15 pm.

The occupational therapist made a very welcome visit today in response to my request for advice on a suitable riser chair for Peter. We need one he can use as an ordinary chair for most of the day, but we also need to have the optional facility for helping to propel Peter into a standing position, without us both having to run the risk of dislocating one or even all of our arms. Katherine, the O.T. is arranging for a specialist in such chairs to come and visit us at home to assess the situation. The O.T. will be in attendance so I am feeling hopeful that the outcome will be good. At a cost of just under seven hundred pounds I shall need to be convinced of the outstanding qualities of any such chair. Peter has had another very good day and is deserving of 10/10.

Saturday August 1st 2009

Rising time - Peter rose from his chair in the Study at 9.15 am.

After an early breakfast Peter went to sleep and slept, for the most part, until half past five in the afternoon. A light lunch was ignored. However, soon after six o'clock he was able to enjoy a substantial dinner, to which I had been able to add the light lunch. It is a process called creative catering and reduces waste to an absolute minimum. There is always the added bonus of extra flavour to whatever is on offer. It will come as no surprise to learn that, in response to the body's request to do some toning of muscles, Peter has spent the evening wandering round the house - downstairs - rattling the doors and indulging in a great deal of totally incomprehensible vocalisation. Some might call it speaking in tongues. I am forced to acknowledge that this level of exposure to nonsense has told me a lot of things about my nature, which I might have preferred not to have been told, although I suspect the moment of truth faces us all from time to time. We just become increasingly skilful in ignoring it. I have noted the self-criticism but am, I suspect, unlikely, unwilling or possibly unable to do much to adjust it. The solution has to be to Keep on Smiling - however silly it seems - that is, if you can identify it. The really silly thing is that I have spent the time, from seven o'clock this morning, wondering if I shall be able to take Peter's clothes from his body, put them in the washing machine and put Peter in the shower. Of course, I could always hose him, fully clad, with warm water. He might then be glad to co-operate. On the other hand he might wander round the house dripping water everywhere, in which case we might have a more irritating situation.

Sunday August 2nd 2009

Rising time 1.45 pm.

Before you start to rejoice over this rising time - and the obvious and accurate assumption that there had been a going-to-bed time - it might be as well to consider the events leading up to the closing of Saturday in this house. After a day of comparative excellence and an apparent willingness to part with his jacket, jersey, shirt tie, shoes and socks,

Peter decided that enough was enough and he decided that aggression - as opposed to discretion - was the better part of valour. To which end he started to practise his air boxing. Of course he is so weak, in the muscle tone sense of the word, that air boxing is reduced to flapping the arms about, but the face is still able to reflect great rage, fury and obstinacy. While trying not to reflect the same emotions in my own face and, having run out of acceptable tactics, I was reminded of the husband of Iris Murdoch, who wrote, in his book, *Iris,* of the time when she was resisting all his attempts to coax her into the shower. He said he had to turn the hose on her - which is exactly what I ventured to suggest yesterday. In the end I was forced to follow his example and turn the shower head on Peter's vest and trousers. He was suitably surprised; in fact he was outraged and started immediately to wander round the house - which was in darkness. I fully expected him to go and sit, in his wet clothes, in the Study, and so make me regret my foolish action. I went upstairs to run a bath and was in the process of adjusting the cold tap when I was conscious of a movement behind me. I then heard, "Hello." It was Peter. I turned and told him I was running his bath. With my back to him I was still aware of what he was doing. First of all he took off the vest and stood in silence. "Good," I said, "Now take off your trousers." This he did and stood, in silence, in his underpants. "Good," I said, "Now take off those pants." This he did and then, most nimbly, climbed into the bath. Seizing the moment - and the sponge - I gave him the soap and started washing him. Then I washed the hair - which caused a great outburst lasting a good five seconds - whereupon Peter started washing himself with great vigour. I went downstairs to sort out the washing. While doing that I heard a sound from the room above - the bathroom - which clearly indicated one thing. I went upstairs, quickly, and found that Peter had stepped out of the bath and was now fully absorbed in drying himself with the towel he had taken from the radiator. Old habits die very hard... He was drying between his toes, behind his knees, between his fingers. All the parts one would normally leave to dry through evaporation. Or am I the only one who does that? Once thoroughly dry, he collected the pyjamas and endeavoured to put his arms through the trouser legs - at which point I intervened. The cleaning of teeth and getting into bed routine was completed very successfully - and Peter seemed very pleased to be able to get into bed. So the day ended very well and I shall have to award the day's outcome a ranking of 9/10 - which is 9 more than it might have been. Today itself has been very good. We shall have to see whether or not my confidence in a trouble-free shower is fully justified. In fact I have decided, now, that we will soon revert to the bath routine. It makes more sense.

Monday August 3rd 2009

Rising time 6.35 pm.

There was an unusual occurrence soon after one o'clock this afternoon. Peter had not eaten his breakfast, so I tried to encourage him to interest himself in the bran flakes and All-bran. He refused to be interested. At half past two I managed to post two pillows behind his back so that he was in a semi-sitting position - in bed, not on the side of the bed. He started to eat his breakfast as I left the bedroom. Not long after, I heard him cross the landing and go into the toilet. When I went upstairs, ten minutes later, he was fast asleep in bed, with the partly eaten bowl of cereal on the tray on the floor. Eventually he managed to finish the breakfast but was in no mood to get dressed. At half past five I took his dinner upstairs, which was when a different pattern of behaviour emerged. He sat on the side of the bed and prepared to eat his dinner. After a minute or so I went downstairs to finish giving Joe and Amber their dinner. After a short while Peter suddenly appeared in the kitchen. He was puzzled by something. I went upstairs and collected his tray of dinner and took it into the Study. His pyjama trousers were now wet so I put a clean pair on him. Within five minutes he was back in the kitchen with more wet trousers. This time I decided to collect up his day clothes and dress him. There was maximum co-operation and he was then able to sit down and eat his dinner.

I have reached the following conclusions about the behaviour:

1. Eating breakfast in the bedroom is acceptable and normal;
2. Eating dinner in the bedroom is not normal and so will be unacceptable;
3. Eating dinner in the Study is acceptable and normal;
4. Eating dinner in the Study while wearing pyjamas is not acceptable;
5. Eating dinner in the Study when correctly dressed is acceptable and normal.

This, I feel, represents what has happened today. Whether the same sequence would apply tomorrow cannot be known, but I am as sure as I can be that he was working towards doing the right thing in the right place - as far as eating food is concerned. Rachel seems very keen for me to start working on introducing Peter to the idea of continence - or more sensibly incontinence - pads. I shall, of course, do my very best to make the introduction the moment such an overture seems appropriate. The theory is beyond contention and I would applaud it from every angle, naturally. But, on the other hand, I am not supposed to be making problems - only solving them. And if there are no problems what shall I do with my large quantity of solutions? They cannot go to waste or lie dormant in the wardrobe. Assuming all goes well in the shower, today will deserve 9/10.

Tuesday August 4th 2009

Rising time 1.45 pm.

Shower time on Monday dashed straight into the world of farce. So much so that today has been cancelled as a sign of. . .something. I will describe the farce before putting up the cancelled sign, to clarify the situation.

Peter seemed willing enough, just before midnight, to go into the shower room and sit down on the chair. He even allowed himself to be parted from all clothes, except for pants and trousers. I turned on the shower and went through the sequence of finding the soap and flannel and pointing to the water. Whereupon he reached into the shower and washed his hands and arms under the running water. Despite several attempts on my part, I failed completely to gain control of the pants and trousers. Realising that the horse was dead, I stopped flogging it, turned off the shower and left the room - carrying the jacket and leaving the rest of the clothes in the washing machine. I then went upstairs to hang the jacket on the dumb valet. Deciding that a second attempt might be worthwhile I went downstairs again, only to find Peter trying to fasten my blue coat which, in an inspired moment of cross-dressing, he had taken from the coat hanger in the utility room and was wearing as his own. Needless to say, I had to mention that the coat belonged to me but that he should continue to wear it, if he so wished. He was still struggling with the zip and the fasteners, but I refrained from offering any assistance. Instead, I had a shower and went to bed, with a glass of the Cassis which Rachel had so kindly brought from France. This was a splendid move because I was quickly able to appreciate the sheer lunacy of the situation - not to mention the cross-dressing. Yes, it would, in a different set of circumstances, have been well worth filming. However we were in our particular set of circumstances, not any other and I had no camera near to hand. I was able to fall asleep very quickly - in our bed, because I forgot to go into the children's room. At around half past three the wanderings started, along with the compulsory switching on of the lights. There were no bulbs in any of the lights so it was rather a waste of energy. Or rather, there was little energy to waste. The gate is only in place if I have personally seen Peter into bed so, of course, he was free to come and go. I was very struck by the almost silent way he was moving around and how he seemed to avoid bumping into anything that made a noise. It was half past four - yes, there had been a lot of to-ing and fro-ing - when I heard Peter come into the bedroom and struggle to unzip the lady's coat he was wearing. The zip was proving to be a little troublesome, but, he persevered, and eventually I heard him throw it, carelessly, to the ground. He then took off the remaining items of clothing, i.e. pants and trousers, and climbed into bed. As soon as I felt sure he was asleep, I went downstairs and turned off the lights in the kitchen and utility rooms and then, thankfully, went back to bed and so to sleep again. When I got up I found my coat had indeed been flung, rudely, to the ground, whereas Peter's trousers had been folded, more or less carefully, and arranged on the dumb valet - who could have had a lot to say if only he had not been so dumb - while the underpants had been folded carefully and placed on the chest of drawers. Never have I seen Peter's clothes tidied away so carefully. This is another skill we might think of cultivating - or not, depending on the time of the day and the lie of the land. The day itself started, with breakfast, at two o'clock, by which time I had him up, dressed and ready to face the day. He could face the day, but Joe and Amber would be returning within minutes, after a happy morning in Manchester with Lillian, and I was determined that nothing would spoil what was left of their day - or mine, for that matter. I wonder if I am right to cancel a day which, on the surface, contains so many elements of the absurd. But we still have tonight to face so, in case we have a re-run, the day will remain cancelled.

Wednesday August 5th 2009

Rising time 1.40 pm.

Peter climbed in and out of the bath last night, having refused to part with his clothing in the shower room. I had left him for a few minutes while I ran a bath and then went downstairs and, to my great relief, he returned, willingly enough, with me. The cancelling of the day was a great success and it may be repeated on some future occasion. Today had been a very good day. He is still responding to bladder messages but the response is increasingly hit and miss - if you will forgive the quip. Thank goodness for Floor Cleaner with added Bleach. Of course, it does mean that the floors are astonishingly clean. A retrospective ranking is 8/10.

Tuesday August 11th 2009

Rising time 2.05 pm.

It may be worth noting that, so far, Peter has not been tempted to tidy up the children's toys, papers and books. Of course, he may have been tempted, but has managed to resist the temptation. Who knows? One important change in the day's routine has been the return to having a bath, instead of a shower, at the end of the day. Certainly it is much easier to part with the clothing. Provided the water is in the bath Peter will sit on the chair and let me take off the jacket, shirt, tie and vest - not forgetting the shoes and socks, which, ideally, come off first. I then help him to stand up and face the bath - containing six inches of water. The days of a deep bath have passed into history - partly to do with the safety element of our favourite friends, Health and Safety. I then stir up the water, again and again, before suggesting that he gets into the bath. At this point he looks at me in a pitying way, as if to say, 'Poor thing. She must think I'm going to get in the bath in my clothes.' To prove me wrong he then takes off the trousers and pants and tries to step gaily into the bath. This is not easy to achieve when he is trying to hang on to the washbasin as well as the handrail on the side of the bath. This sort of manoeuvre really demands a scissor-like response on the part of the legs in order for the body to reach the water. However, it is managed, somehow, and I can then reasonably expect Peter to wash himself and, eventually, try and get out of the bath. I have found that wrapping a dry towelling flannel round each of the bath hand rails provides a non-slip grip which makes it a little easier for Peter to get out of the bath. At the moment he manages this by pulling himself into a kneeling position. He can then, generally, pull himself into a standing position. Provided I am there to provide back-up support it works, and drying the body and putting on pyjamas can follow. It is somewhat curious when one considers that the whole point of using the shower was to solve the problem of getting out of the bath. Perhaps, somewhere along the line, I have misread the signs. Or perhaps Peter found that he preferred having a bath. If he did think that, then the brain is still functioning at some level. Ah well, I do not suppose we shall find the answer to that question. The day deserves a ranking of 10/10.

Chapter Three - Some successful problem solving

Friday August 14th 2009

Rising time - a truly shocking 11.30 am.

This was deliberate because the occupational therapist was expecting to visit, at midday, with a provider of chairs for people with various needs. Briefly, I was delighted to be advised that Peter's existing chair can be adapted, by the fitting of a motor to the underside of the chair, to raise the occupant, by means of a cleverly designed lever, to an almost standing position. The chair will be adapted next Thursday and we shall try it out for one month before deciding whether or not it is suitable for our particular needs. In view of the shock Peter experienced, in his early rising, the least we can do is award the day another 10/10.

Monday August 24th 2009

Rising time 1.55 pm.

We are now the proud owners of a customized inclining chair. Phil, the chair fitter, arrived promptly at one o'clock and spent a mere twenty minutes fitting a substantial motor to the under-surface of Peter's armchair which will, I am sure, solve all present and future difficulties associated with getting in and out of the chair. Joe and Amber carried out several tests and declared themselves satisfied with the results. I have not yet tested the chair fully, as Peter has spent most of the time sitting in it. If this works, as I am sure it will, then I shall feel this qualifies as an investment as far as the quality of Peter's life is concerned. If I do not have to drag him out of the chair, then there should be a reduction in hassle and negative thoughts. After all, we have no means of telling how negative are his thoughts on my ability and skill in heaving bodies from chairs.

The day has been quietly successful. There has been an increase in Peter's level of frailty. He has been very tottery this evening, but I do think part of that may be due to the fact that he has spent a long time standing up, folding cloths and arranging them round the kitchen. It is the standing that could be a factor. I have also noticed a slight swelling of his ankles, which may be associated with a surfeit of standing. Let us award the day a ranking of 9/10.

Thursday August 27th 2009

Rising time 1.45 pm.

The chair took off at the end of the day. When it became obvious that Peter was not going to leave his comfortable chair willingly, I resorted to the remote control. He did not appear to register anything at all. There was no sign of surprise, pleasure or consternation when his chair started to move in an upward direction and so cause him to lean forward. I stopped the process when he seemed to be in an appropriate position, before moving in front of him and taking his hands so that he could stand up. It was so easy. I realise that, although I thought the chair had been adapted for Peter's benefit, in reality it has been adapted for my benefit - which has surprised me. But I shall see a great improvement in my arms from now on. I shall rank the day as 7/10.

Monday August 31st 2009

Rising time - a reluctant 3.05 pm, even though it is Bank Holiday Monday.

Perhaps it has been a good thing that the rising time was so late, because Peter's restlessness and wandering around has been considerable. I shall feel the benefit of the chair when it is time to go to bed, as Peter is now soundly asleep and will, I am sure, need the chair to remind him as to how he should set about standing up.

What have I learnt this month? Several important lessons have been learned.

1. It is well worth keeping the routine of bathing rather than showering, as there are useful strategies which can be employed as far as undressing is concerned. Peter makes more sense of what is required when he can see the water in the bath. If he is reluctant to take off his jacket this can usually be achieved by standing him in front of the bath, swirling the water round and round, and then repeating the suggestion of unbuttoning the jacket. If he is wobbly then it is worth letting him sit down once the shirt has been removed. If the trousers cause a problem then, again, facing the bath seems to remind him that it is safe to unfasten his belt and nothing too dreadful will happen.

2. All upstairs doors need to be either locked or securely jammed during the night, as Peter can go on night patrol and then there can be inconvenient consequences. I am now keeping the doors locked and/or closed whenever I am out of the house. All rubbish bins, plant pots and other convenient-looking receptacles will have to be kept well out of reach. Eventually, I am sure, it will appear normal to keep one's tall swing-bin on the draining board. Of course this only applies during wandering hours. Such sources of temptation are perfectly safe all the time Peter is safely in bed.

3. Diluted bleach in a Mr Muscle spray bottle is as effective - and less expensive - as any floor cleaner after mopping up operations. The number of times one has to mop up these days means that the floors must be almost germ-free.

4. Do not underestimate the brain-numbing effect of constant supervision. I am most grateful to Charles for lending me two splendid books on *Understanding Music* and *Harmonisation of the Bach Chorales*. Pedalling is good for muscle tone, writing is good for relaxation but, in the absence of sensible conversation, I am hoping that perhaps ten or twenty minutes spent in some demanding activity will control, or at least reduce, excessive mental, if not cerebral, atrophy. No exams needed to prove whether or not I have understood what I have been reading about. Thank you, Charles.

5. At the moment the only place where it is possible to change out of wet pyjama trousers is in the bedroom - sitting on the bed. This is where he dresses in the morning and so it seems to be considered acceptable to change from one set of pyjama trousers to another without having to resort to aggressive behaviour.

6. After nine years of grappling with this disease I am still surprised by some aspects of Peter's understanding and behaviour - which seems to suggest that the more we *think* we know the less we *really* know. Which is just one of life's little challenges!

7. When you think the brain has given up all attempts it will surprise you by causing some unexpected reaction. So, do not fall into the trap of assuming that your spoken thoughts and any other observations will not be understood. You never know when that cunning little brain is going to spring into life and action. The understanding may be very brief but it should always be positive. So keep your annoyance, unworthy and pernicious comments to yourself. Telling a friend will help neither you nor the friend. Sometimes it is as well to ask God what He thinks He's up to. If you can carry on, then you may presume to have had some sort of response. . .perhaps!

The day ends as 9/10.

September 1st 2009

Rising time 1.35 pm.

Today has been the last day of the summer holidays as far as the children being together is concerned. Amber goes back to School tomorrow - Wednesday - William and Molly return next Wednesday and Joe returns a week on Thursday. We were fortunate in having a lovely sunny morning so that some more energetic and imaginative games - involving the Beanies - could be played and enjoyed. I think each child has benefited from the interaction with the cousins and, I have to say, I have greatly enjoyed the many lovely days we have shared over these last six weeks. Peter has not found the presence of the children at all disturbing, as far as I can tell. There were occasions, several years ago, when he did seem to be bothered by, and somewhat resentful of, their presence but there is no evidence whatsoever of such feelings now.

The motorised chair is proving to be a great success and I do wonder whether Peter has actually registered something different about his chair. It may be my imagination of course, but, last night, I had the definite impression that, as I went behind the chair, he was actually waiting for something to happen. There seemed to be a very slight trace of anticipation on his face. Keeping the upstairs doors locked - with the exception of the toilet - also seems to be paying dividends. The puddles in the night are certainly smaller and are, of course, confined to the room containing the toilet. I wonder why it has taken me so long to work out this simple expedient. Another fact I have noted is that he does not attempt to get back into bed if the pyjama trousers are wet. (He either stands by the bed or sits on the edge.) This may seem obvious to you and me, but it suggests to me that he is registering wetness when wearing thin cotton pyjamas, which he does not appear to register when wearing his two layers of long johns and his smart trousers - which I am now washing every single day. The pyjamas must feel much colder than his day clothes, which fact he must be noticing and which, in turn, must reflect some brain activity. I am going to move out of the Study as I am proving to be something of a problem for him. He cannot settle with his book or the lever arch file, so I shall move out. The day ranks as 9/10.

Wednesday September 2nd 2009

Rising time 1.45 pm.

Peter has enjoyed a calm and peaceful day - which has been of considerable benefit to us all. The Police Choir meets tonight so it will be interesting to see what Rachel has to say after her return to duty. My report today is very brief - mainly due to a shortage of time but also because, so far, there has been nothing new to mention. The day deserves 8/10.

> "Life has resumed its normal pattern after the summer holiday. Dad was settled and sleeping when I arrived. Obviously he had given up on the chair lift. He has been sleeping all the evening. Took coffee in at 9. He seems to be leaning to the right (was that the honeysuckle or the bindweed?) and looks very lost. As you say, Mother, there is a constant low-level tremor in the hands now, with intermittent jolts. Again, his temperature seems up a little bit, but breathing is all as it should be. These are all the marks of the additional frailty you have been noting, I suppose."

Sunday September 13th 2009

Rising time 3.50 pm.

After an outrageous night, during which Peter refused to be parted from his wet clothes, I was driven from my side of the bed and eventually went to sleep in the children's room - and what a splendid and refreshing sleep it turned out to be. I have cancelled the night and given it a zero ranking minus (at least 4) but it would not be fair to carry the displeasure - although sorely tempted - into the next twenty four hours.

Monday September 14th 2009

Rising time 2.45 pm.

Peter has spent most of the day asleep - either in bed or in the chair. Kathryn, the occupational therapist, called in to see the wonder of the rising chair. It was good to see her reaction to a new product to add to her list of helpful gadgets. She did not know of the existence of a motor which could be attached to a chair, which would then be converted to a Riser Chair. I am sure it could be of great interest to several other people in situations similar to our own. Peter's tremor is rather more marked today. He is very tottery on his feet and I feel more and more certain that a lot of the puddle problems are linked to shaky hands and, consequently, a less than certain aim. I did find myself wondering how much longer he would be able to manage to climb the stairs. It is a slow and laborious job at the moment - which does not mean that he is likely to stop in the near future, but I do just wonder. Today is deserving of 9/10.

Tuesday September 15th 2009

Rising time 2.10 pm.

Peter is presenting now as a very peaceful, calm and contented person. I really do not think he is experiencing anything to upset him or make him wish to be somewhere else. I would say that, at the moment, he is 'content with his lot.' We may not be, but maintaining the status quo is certainly nowhere near as challenging, physically, as heretofore. Anticipating possible areas of confusion, and keeping a very close watch on both Peter and the situation make up most of the workload. Domestic routines are second nature and so do not cause any problems. The washing machine and dryer continue to be great allies - and having a comfortable bath is manageable. I bought a rather interesting bath seat, two or three years ago, which is now proving most useful. Peter can, as he tries to get out of the bath, raise himself enough for me to slide the seat under his bottom, so that he can sit and draw breath before standing up and climbing out of the bath. So, with the seat and the grab rails we have an excellent support system. The only thing we are short of in this house is a set of parallel bars! I am sure we could fix such things should the need for exercise become really desperate. Peter is sleeping, I would say, for a good nineteen hours of each day so the muscle tone problem is becoming more academic. The chair is still a wonderful device - and a cause for great rejoicing.

Sunday September 27th 2009

Rising time 1.35 pm.

Peter was still asleep and breakfast still uneaten when I returned from church this morning - just before one o'clock. It seemed a good idea to organise the dressing as soon as he had eaten his breakfast. In fact it *was* a good idea. Peter is so calm and peaceful these days: I can scarcely credit how we have managed over these last few years. The absence of distress, frustration, anger and panic has made a tremendous difference to the lives of those of us trying to keep Peter's life within the realms of normality. This is probably an exaggerated claim but I do feel that life has improved since we, as a family, have learned that whatever goes on inside these four walls is entirely normal

- for us! This is not unreasonable as we are the ones dealing with the situation - and the ones accepting the situation. The day ranks as 8/10.

Tuesday September 29th 2009

Rising time 2.05 pm.

I have come to the conclusion that the way Peter is living his life, at the moment, is an example of how people should be allowed to live, when their freedom and ability to fit into what we might regard as general or even normal life has been removed from them. Of course, it is only possible now because he has passed through the agonies of knowledge, leading to frustration and resentment, and has reached a plateau of peace and contentment. He is free to creep about at will, to get up when he feels he can, he has the food he likes in a way he can enjoy it and has a lovely comfortable bed. Peter looks so calm and peaceful, so at ease with himself and relaxed in living life at his own pace, that it is not easy to see how his quality of life, on this earth, could be greatly improved. I realise, of course, that this may serve as a catalyst to some new and possibly extraordinary behaviour - but I will run the risk and accept the challenge, if and when it comes. Ranking has to be 9/10.

Monday October 5th 2009

Rising time 2.15 pm.

Impeccable behaviour has not been the order of the day today. The dressing routine was disturbed when, quite suddenly, the clean dry underpants became wet and in need of instant removal. This requires some element of co-operation on the part of the wearer. There was no such element. Instead there was a loud and vigorous protest. After resisting the temptation to protest, myself, on a loud and vigorous basis, I ordered Peter to behave himself and stand still! He did. But, although he appears to have forgotten the episode within seconds, it leaves the carer feeling somewhat bemused - which is counter-productive - so the best reaction to have is to regard the incident as dull and tedious - which it is - and then get on with the next stage as efficiently as possible. The work has suddenly piled up so I shall rank the day as 8/10 and prepare for the morrow.

Friday October 9th 2009

Rising time 12 35 pm.

The end of this month of October will mark the end of the second year of this particular account of our attempts in coming to terms with Alzheimer's disease. Well, we have indeed Kept Going and, as a result, learnt many things. One of the many things I have noticed, over the last few weeks, is that there has been such a reduction in Peter's involvement with the world outside, or beyond, Alzheimer's disease. It has been so reduced that many days pass without there being any apparent connection on his part. Perhaps it is time to take a more clinical view of what is happening. Put in its simplest form - nothing happens. Nothing is said. Nothing changes any more. Today will rank as 9/10, but I shall concentrate on a possible change in form for November and subsequent months.

He was well satisfied with his work today and searched for other jobs in the kitchen. The rest of the day has been quiet and peaceful. There was a flurry of activity, lasting about ten minutes, when Peter discovered the Playmobil fire engine and seven Playmobil characters. The engine was obviously in need of attention and the figures were in need of being lined up. Peter greatly enjoyed this activity and was relieved when he managed to make the last figure stand to attention. It was obviously regarded as a job well done. Order out of chaos. The day deserves 9/10.

Friday October 16th 2009

Rising time 2.10 pm.

Because of certain events taking place at the wrong time and different people being in the house at the wrong time, Peter has found it necessary to emerge from his self-imposed hibernation. This has resulted in an extraordinary interest in the door handle of the oven, my new book of songs by Purcell, a desire to move his chair from its perfectly suitable place to an entirely unsuitable place, and then to sit in a beanbag next to the piano. The Study chair is very heavy and I am surprised at the way he perseveres in his removal attempts. Of course I should have noted the slightly unusual beginning to the day. I was helping Peter to dress when I heard the telephone ringing. I left him, briefly to pull up his smart long johns - fully expecting that he would still be struggling when I returned. How foolish I am. On my return I found him wearing his jacket and attempting to plait the laces of his left shoe. Now I know, from experience, that it is not possible to fit the trousers onto the legs if a shoe is in the way. The only thing to do is to remove the shoe, put on the trousers and re-fit the shoe. This presented a serious problem for Peter because, as far as he was concerned, his shoe was on his foot and that was where it was staying. Now, I am all for independence and free, or even self, expression, but, another big But, the thought of Peter spending the remains of today in shirt, tie, jersey, jacket, a left shoe and a pair of long johns could never meet with my acceptance, never mind approval. The more he resisted my attempts to possess the shoe, the clearer appeared this image of anything but sartorial elegance. In the end the shoelace broke into two pieces, which caught Peter's keen attention and interest. With a cunning sleight of hand I gave him the broken lace and secured possession of the shoe. The whole episode was over and I could thread the trousers over the legs and then put on the shoes. It has to be said that the shoes do not exactly match because it was necessary to move quickly. Fortunately he was able to be fitted with a left and a right shoe, so it could have been a great deal worse. Both shoes are black but one has some decorative stitching on the top of the shoe. Who will worry? Not I. Instead I shall ignore the stalking and interference this evening and attribute Peter's behaviour to the fact that I am doing housework this evening instead of being out of sight. Although, of course, I would be out of sight if he would only stay in the Study and read his current book - an Ordnance Survey book on Wales. He has been busy examining it for the last week, but there is still a long way to go before he has exhausted its potential. The day can have 7/10 - in recognition of the trick with the lace.

I am going to take one last trip down Memory Lane. I am going back to Manchester and to the time the Retail Park was doing its utmost to buy part of the School playing field, in order to increase its car parking space. I held out for as long as possible but perhaps I should have taken more notice of my eleven year old boys. . .

Here I am in the Retail Park, in the early days of its creation. One of the first shops was called Children's World - which name our children took very much to heart. Some very fine trolleys had been provided for customers to use, in the normal shopping trolley fashion. Some people used them to fill the canal at the back of school and others used them as vehicles, to be driven at speed all over the school grounds. The managing director then thought of a brilliant way of recovering his lost trolleys. He made it known that he would pay £1 for the return of each and every trolley found any distance from his premises. My boys were delighted and set themselves the task of finding ways of recovering lost or stolen trolleys. Their idea was brilliant in its simplicity. One group of boys would steal the trolleys and another group of boys would return the trolleys. The amount paid out by Children's World would be shared equally between the two groups. Due to the incredible innocence of Children's World my boys were able to acquire much more money than they deserved for their idea. I had to speak to them about it, in case they thought life was always going to be that easy...

Tuesday October 20th 2009

Rising time 12.05 pm.

Totally shocking! I arrived home at twelve noon to find Peter wandering round the house and wearing very wet pyjamas. Of Cousin John, who was acting as honorary guardian, there was no sign. He had abandoned his post and gone off - to return at five past six, having toured Hyde, Buxton, Macclesfield and Poynton - courtesy of his free bus pass - and having enjoyed most of the day!

The Postman had failed to deliver a parcel at eleven o'clock, so John was obviously not around then. Something must have distracted Peter at some point, because coming downstairs has not been on his Agenda of Exciting Things To Do for some long time. He spent the afternoon asleep in the Study and is now, at nine o'clock, full of life. It has proved to be too exciting for Cousin John, as he has thrown in his sponge and gone to his room.

The speaking in tongues is very evident tonight but, as I am no nearer understanding any of it, I shall rank the day as 8/10 - because we have all done our best.

Sunday October 25th 2009

Rising time 1.45 pm.

Having spent a week showing how balanced and peaceful he could be, Peter has chosen his evening to show the reverse side of both coins. However, I shall diagnose a condition of attention seeking behaviour and reserve any judgement/condemnation until a future date - like Wednesday afternoon. I can find no satisfactory explanation for the fact that, on getting out of the bath, completing the drying and the putting on of the pyjama jacket, he should then have an overwhelming need to toss the towel into the bath. I pointed out that this was no way for a gentleman to behave. He beamed and, to all intents and purposes, agreed with my comment. I dare say I would be advised by experts to have refrained from comment. Had I been an expert I might even have gone along with the advice. Happily I am not an expert and so am still capable of reacting, perhaps mildly, to certain behaviour. We can move on from there, rule it out of the equation, or put it in brackets, and rank the day as 8/10.

Friday October 30th 2009

Rising time 1.35 pm.

If things go according to plan, today will be the penultimate day of the Keeping Going record. I have not made a final decision about reaching any sort of conclusion, but, as Peter spends so much time sleeping in bed or resting/dozing in the Study, I am not exactly certain how best to preserve some sort of record of his daily life. The quality of his life is still, by any standard, at a very satisfactory level. He does spend many of his waking hours with his eyes closed. Of course, it is not always obvious that he is asleep. I am working on the principle that closed eyes indicate a withdrawal from an energetic interaction with what one might describe as daily life. But, having said that, he has busied himself with the kitchen and its contents. As with the very young child, I have been forced to acknowledge that constant supervision - and appropriate intervention - will, generally, greatly reduce toileting problems and puddles. In the meantime today will rank as 9/10.

Chapter Four - In conclusion

Saturday October 31ˢᵗ 2009

Rising time 2.05 pm.

It is two years since I started recording our experiences, and now may be a good time to evaluate the worth of the many thousands of words to the family as a whole.

I could repeat many of the points I have already made, but the most significant realisation, from my own point of view, is the pace of the disease. I suspect that an initial response on seeing Peter, after an interval of perhaps a few months, would be that there had been rather rapid decline in his condition. Reading the events noted, possibly in batches of three months, would suggest that rather than the decline being rapid, the decline has followed a systematic and steady path at a relentless but consistent pace. This might suggest that the disease has progressed in a calculated and perhaps inevitable manner. Bearing in mind that each individual person will be experiencing symptoms which may be peculiar to that individual, there must still be a general pattern for the progress of the disease. So where does leave that us? Peter is still here, but seems unaware of most of the life he is living. From the family's perspective we have realised that accepting what goes on in our house as being *entirely normal* goes a long way to making what goes on *acceptable*. Acceptance results in a reduction of frustration and annoyance.

I am considering different ways of continuing the monitoring of Peter's condition and behaviour, and am working on the idea of making a daily comparison - in a very brief way - of the situation on, for example,

November 1st 2009 and the situation as recorded on the same dates in 2007 and 2008. This could be recorded on a daily basis, which may then give us a clearer idea of what has gone on over the two-year period. It is an idea which appeals to me and one which could be very helpful in understanding the nature of Alzheimer's disease. The recording of our experiences, thus far, has been immensely valuable to us and, if the new idea of making comparisons works in the way I expect, then we should all be that little bit nearer understanding what Peter is doing with his brain.

One new development has taken place in the last few minutes. Peter has been looking at the book on Archbishop Cranmer and has been pointing at the front picture and trying to articulate some thoughts. I was obviously not paying sufficient attention while I was writing this Conclusion, so, for the first time, in my experience, he put the book on his knee and clapped both hands very vigorously. I stopped typing and looked over at Peter. He picked up the book and started again with some explanation about the picture. I have never known him try and attract attention in this way - but it certainly worked. He has now lost interest in Thomas Cranmer and reverted to staring in to space. One thing which has never changed has been his ability to respond to a smile.

In conclusion I feel certain that Peter's lifestyle suits him as well as it possibly can, and that he is shielded from most levels of frustration. Because of this I would like to think that he remains in control of the positive elements of his behaviour - or, at least, his reactions to situations. Are we justified in thinking that, because a response may seem inappropriate or irrational, a person with any form of dementia is not capable of an appropriate or rational response? Perhaps Peter is understanding more than I think and is planning a response to a given situation. Perhaps that response is then distorted and made to appear as a no-response - or even a negative response. Perhaps we should not assume that a person with dementia is failing to understand what is being required. Perhaps that person is giving instructions which are being misinterpreted. I have decided to assume that Peter understands what is required, but is prevented, by Alzheimer's, from making the appropriate response. That leaves us with the question: Will this approach create a more understanding and reasonable carer? In answer to that question I am brought back to the tremendous importance of the need for the carer to be free to build whatever life seems appropriate, as much around the carer's needs as the needs of the person cared for. No two situations will be the same. One person's idea of successful respite may not be at all suitable for another person, but the respite does need to suit the carer, rather than being something another well-meaning person/organisation feels will be helpful to that person. To know yourself and your own needs is not, by definition, a sign of selfishness. It could, indeed, be a certain sign of effectiveness in a situation which is totally devoid of any sort of sense. Buying in help may be an excellent idea, but, if it is not the help the carer actually needs, it could well be a waste of money, which may not be easy to replace.

It may even be more useful to remember a phrase you may have had to learn in childhood:

"If your face wants to smile - let it. If it doesn't - make it."

This now brings us back to October 31st 2009 and the ending of this particular stage in our relationship with Alzheimer's disease. Perhaps it will lead to a conviction that, somehow, order will continue to be created from the current chaos of our lives.

Perhaps the time of reading, writing and doing - during this two year period in the life we continue live with Alzheimer's disease - will remind us of the truth contained within a well-known saying of

Confucius, the renowned Chinese philosopher, teacher and politician, who was born in the year 551 BC. He said:

"I hear and I forget. I read and I remember. I do and I understand."

How true this has been for us. It is in the reality of living with Alzheimer's that we have come to recognize, but not necessarily understand, *something* of what goes on and *something* of how best to manage some of the challenges. There is still a great deal of work to be done if we are to make sense of this disease. I hope, in my sequel to *Order out of Chaos,* to continue my search for different strands of knowledge and information. More understanding may be helpful to us in coping with what we have undertaken to do. Peter, along with all sufferers from Alzheimer's disease, will continue to need sustained love, care and attention in order to have some protection from the cruel reality of his own relationship with the disease. We learn about it as he lives it - which is the more difficult I wonder.

If you have travelled with me I wish you peace and every blessing in what you are striving to do.

Made in the USA
Charleston, SC
09 January 2015